A SALVO FOR AFRICA

Books by Douglas Oliver

Oppo Hectic (Ferry Press, 1969)

The Harmless Building (Grosseteste and Ferry Presses, 1973)

In the Cave of Suicession (Street Editions, 1974)

The Diagram Poems (Ferry Press, 1979)

The Infant and the Pearl (Silver Hounds for Ferry Press, 1985)

Kind: Collected Poems (Allardyce, Barnett, Publishers, 1987)

Poetry and Narrative in Performance (Macmillan/St Martin's Press, 1989)

Three Variations on the Theme of Harm (Paladin, 1990)

The Scarlet Cabinet, with Alice Notley (Scarlet Editions, NY, 1992)

Penniless Politics (Bloodaxe Books, 1994)

Penguin Modern Poets 10, with Denise Riley & Iain Sinclair
    (Penguin, 1996)

Selected Poems (Talisman House, 1996)

etruscan reader VIII, with Tina Darragh & Randloph Healy
    (etruscan books, 1998)

A Salvo for Africa (Bloodaxe Books, 2000)

DOUGLAS OLIVER

A Salvo for Africa

BLODAXE BOOKS

ISBN: 1 85224 475 5

First published 2000 by
Bloodaxe Books Ltd,
P.O. Box 1SN,
Newcastle upon Tyne NE99 1SN.

Bloodaxe Books Ltd acknowledges
the financial assistance of Northern Arts.

Cover printing by J. Thomson Colour Printers Ltd, Glasgow.

Printed in Great Britain by
Cromwell Press Ltd, Trowbridge, Wiltshire.

Speechmaker, you speak too late. Just a little time ago you would have been able to believe in your speech, now you no longer can. For, a moment ago, you saw as I did, that the State is no longer led; the stokers still pile in the coal, but the leaders have now only the semblance of control over the madly racing machines. And in this moment, as you speak, you can hear as I do that the levers of economics are beginning to sound in an unusual way; the masters smile at you with superior assurance, but death is in their hearts. They tell you they suited the apparatus to the circumstances, but you notice that from now on they can only suit themselves to the apparatus – so long, that is to say, as it permits them. Their speakers teach you that economics is entering on the State's inheritance, but you know that there is nothing to inherit except the tyranny of the exuberantly growing It, under which the I, less and less able to master, dreams on that it is the ruler.

MARTIN BUBER, *I and Thou*

ACKNOWLEDGEMENTS

I should like to thank Isabelle Gillette of the Groupes de Femmes pour l'Abolition des Mutilations Sexuelles (GAMS) in Paris for her courtesy and help, Ken Mackenzie for reading the manuscript in draft and saving me from various errors, and Greg Chamberlain for keeping me documented.

These poems have appeared, without the commentaries, as follows: 'Our Family Is Full of Problems', 'The Unseeing Drum', 'The Borrowed Bow', 'The King's Garden', 'The Infibulation Ceremony', 'The Childhood Map' and 'The New Medicine' in *Penguin Modern Poets 10* (1996); 'A Salvo for Malawi' in *Conductors of Chaos*, ed. Iain Sinclair (Picador, 1996); 'A Salvo for Malawi', 'The Unseeing Drum', 'A Woman in Ethiopia' and 'The Infibulation Ceremony' in the *London Review of Books*; 'The Borrowed Bow' in *The New Republic*; 'The Herb' in *Parataxis*; 'The New Medicine' and 'The King's Garden' in *New Statesman & Society*; 'Our Family Is Full of Problems', 'High Priest's Son', 'The Childhood Map', 'Protection from the Heat', 'The Lurch into Neutrality' and 'Soot' (also in *Japan Environment Monitor*) in *Active in Airtime*; 'Our Generation' in *The World*; 'The Childhood Map' in *New American Writing*; 'The Birds of Kenya' in *Pharos*. My thanks to the editors concerned.

A Salvo for Africa is Book I of *Arrondissements*, a series of books on themes arising from life in the arrondissements of Paris.

CONTENTS

The Dumb Barter

In 1993, when this book was begun, Britain and America had turned their attention away from Africa and towards more favoured aid and investment areas in the Middle East, Far East, and Latin America. More than a decade of Thatcherite-Majorite policies in Britain and Reagan-Bush Republicanism had seen Africa regarded as a hopeless sink into which aid money disappeared.

At that time, while the GATT talks were finalising the shape of the World Trade Organisation, global free marketing seemed a battle conducted between Europe, the US, and the richer parts of Asia. The 'Triad', as it's called.

Africa, which contains 18 of the world's 20 poorest countries, stood more at risk from the new economics than any other continent. During the final talks that set up the WTO, African delegates sat tight-mouthed to see discussions swamped by US-French quarrels over soy beans and over their respective movie industries.

Our greatest cruelties often arise from a failure to imagine. That's why poetry often has to do with politics and why these British poems have to do with Africa.

My original version of this book was a *cri du cœur*. For God's sake look again at this continent. Africa must sort its own problems out, but don't turn away like that. Stop sucking out its wealth through the long tubes of debt running into the very stomachs of its countries. Make World Bank/IMF structural adjustment programmes more flexible so that nations are not destabilised by them. Don't trust free global trading to operate as a fairy godmother – it has enough contradictions in it already, even for wealthy Triad countries, and inexorably increases gaps between rich and poor. Watch out for international patent protection of genetic plant and animal technology. Monitor transnational companies, for they are trying to influence global trade policy to help them infiltrate developing nations and absorb part of their sovereignty. Above all, support indigenous peacekeeping moves in Africa.

Poetry has a long take-off roll. In the last two or three years, Triad countries have been paying new attention to Africa at last. My original *cri du cœur* has become a call from a bandwagon. If so, I'm delighted, because I'm not claiming prophetic powers: all my themes were in the air long ago, awaiting their political moment. They weren't in British poetry, that was all. So grave are the issues that I use a direct, undissembled voice, though one that exposes its deficiencies: my more avant-garde poetic styles are not appropriate here.

Since my original draft, I have had to update my political commentaries; but the poems, by their nature, haven't needed more than slight stylistic revision.

With one particular exception, a tragic one. In 'Foreigners and Sudan' I've had to change the number of war-related deaths from one million to two – Sudan's war has been the most neglected human catastrophe of its size since WWII.

Why poetry on such topics? Poets become foolish when they suggest amateurish solutions to mighty problems; they become exploitative if they parade their compassion; and if they sneer at politicians' difficulties from safe avant-garde margins that's rather despicable. More interestingly, a poem can re-imagine a dulled-over political issue for us, making it lively.

The suffering of the African continent has been, for the Western citizen, one of those dull issues. "Compassion fatigue" is the cliché; and in Britain, France, Germany, Belgium, and Italy it's also "colonial guilt fatigue". But it's not just an old colonial thing: the rich, just by being rich, are always in debt to the poor and do nothing for them that isn't a return on this day-to-day obligation.

Developing nations throughout the world owe some $2.2 trillion, and the interest charges transport their wealth to the North. The World Bank in a typical year makes more than $1 billion for itself and nearly $7 billion for its bondholders, with more than twice that amount retained as assets accumulated from debts serviced by the world's poorer countries.

The average African today eats 10 percent less than 20 years ago. A western child will consume and pollute more in its lifetime than 50 children from its poorest nations. Galloping population growth or falling childbirths under economic stagnation, unbalanced cropping, droughts, famines, reliance on loans and food aid, rapacious and dictatorial regimes, lack of education or medical care, wars, massacres, genocide…these are familiar stories.

Large-scale loan schemes have proved enormously wasteful, with foreign-trained experts baffled by African soils, pests, eating or marketing habits, administrative corruption, and lack of trained maintenance personnel. Western consortia have picked up the contracts; local elites have profited too; but not the poor.

Emergency aid also has had a chequered, if praiseworthy, record. While international agencies have saved lives, they have sometimes had to take sides in prolonged wars (beginning in famine-struck Biafra in the 1960s), and have helped governments to continue policies that exacerbated the emergency in the first place.

The spread of AIDS through Africa fills us with a sadness almost too deep to indulge. In sub-Saharan Africa, 34 million people are HIV-infected, with women in a majority. In Zimbabwe 40 percent of adults are HIV positive and because of AIDS in Botswana life expectancy has fallen from 70 to 40 years. South Africa is said to have 14 percent HIV infection. The development of cheaper, generic medicines for Third World countries is being blocked by the new international patenting regulations.

Economic and democratic success in centre, west, and north Africa remains very patchy. A controversial devaluation of the French exchange franc, aided by rising world commodity prices, has reportedly revived productivity in some Francophone West African nations. But large areas of Africa are in civil convulsion. Among other struggles, neighbouring countries have dangerous disputes about which side "peacekeeping" should support in the Congo, Angola, or Sierra Leone. UN emergency food aid has had to be supplied to these countries, to Congo/Brazzaville, Burundi, Tanzania, Guinea Bissau, and to other regions.

Refugee numbers on the continent have risen from one million in 1997 to five million today.

Easy to fall into despair and see new or continued wars or conflict negotiations in countries whose governmental structures are authoritarian or disastrous or religiously doctrinaire or infected by politically-ambitious rebellions: Angola, Somalia, Liberia, the two Congos, Rwanda and Burundi, Sierra Leone, Mauritania, Eritrea, Ethiopia and Sudan. For a bewildering number of reasons, nine neighbouring countries around the Congo are participating in 'Africa's World War', in which tens of thousands of people have died in the months following notorious massacres, with the Congo's mineral riches in the heart of the conflict.

Refusing to despair, from my Paris flat I write these poems about Africa.

Six years ago, my theme was, 'Global trading may leave Africa in the lurch'. To update, do I simply substitute "is leaving" for "may leave"? Nowadays, I find that question immensely hard to answer.

In truth, no one really knows how deregulation will go, long-term. It's an immensely powerful wild card slipped into the international game. Plausibly, in Northern nations it will increase unemployment and inequality as the low-skilled jobs are shipped out to sweated labour in East Asia or South America. Most African countries probably won't benefit in the shorter term: shattered communities, lack of technical expertise, and incompatibility with white social patterns will not easily provide the docile, efficient labour forces that our neo-colonialist transnationals want.

However – and my poems have to wrestle with this irony – the worst-run African nations will have to ensure more democracy and better performance or investors will continue to shy off. Most ironic of all, to the extent that Africans do become sweated labour for the North their actual incomes may somewhat improve.

A non-expert can't convincingly discuss the stabilising effect or otherwise of World Bank/IMF "restructuring" programmes, with their anti-inflationary, pro-privatisation, and pro-foreign investment bias. The bankers point to such countries as Ghana, Ivory Coast, Botswana, and Mozambique as successes – though surely other stabilising factors (improved markets for national exports, and so on) have been also in play.

Critics of "restructuring" retort that in many countries it has helped to shrink indigenous agriculture and enterprise, failed to stimulate exports, strangled already feeble welfare policies, let the rich and the corrupt prosper, hit the middle classes, borne down on the a poverty unimaginable by Western standards, struck at health care and education, and dangerously destabilised societies sometimes already in the grip of political crises.

Neither side can be fully trusted and most statistics have political agendas behind them. Responding to criticism, the World Bank now tries to make loan programmes more responsive to social conditions and to link aid to stable democracy.

African national leaderships, improve as they must, will be able to do little without debt relief. At last, a campaign to 'break the chains', as *The Guardian* puts it, is gaining momentum. Triad nations are at last hestitantly moving towards not "debt rescheduling", but "debt forgiveness", the most exciting prospect of all.

On UN figures, Africa is showing a 4.5 percent growth, or perhaps 3.8 percent taking 1998 figures – either way, faster than any other world region. But this is from a low base and international investment is slow to follow, even in South Africa.

Irretrievably behind in genetic engineering and other technology, desperately needing improved crop and animal varieties, poorer African countries will be cast at the mercy of Triad technology and economic power for the foreseeable future. Major transnationals, trapped in a furious international race to patent genetically manipulated organisms, will have little sympathy to spare.

The smaller nations may have to sell their souls to entice the major Northern investors and trade monopolies at all.

Free traders shrug that the nation-state will inevitably wither away under global economic pressure. A good thing too, not least in Africa's uneasy, artificially-created countries. Diehards even see transnational firms as the saviours rather than the aggressors. 'It is possible to argue that the multinational corporation is the most powerful social glue left in a world sundered by unbridled nationalism, ethnic strife and an absence of ideology,' cooed *Newsweek* a while back.

The revolution of capitalists destroys the state *apparat*: Marxism in reverse.

You don't have to be a nation-stater to think indigenous peoples should decide their own future. And the continent is too various and too rocky in its fortune for confidence in any prescription, free-market or interventionist.

My narrative will move partly geographically, partly historically, and partly thematically across Africa. Much of the continent's extent and several of its nations will be covered, rich and poor, Muslim, Christian, animist, post-Marxist, post-World Bankist. One or two former French, Belgian, German, and Portuguese possessions will be included as well as British to give at least some sense of how Africa remains part of our human locality.

When I mention my project to Africanist friends they immediately ask: 'Have you ever been to Africa?' 'No,' I reply. 'Neither have most people I know. That's just why our imagination is failing.'

Africans are set within their own situation where their voices alone count. There's nothing I can tell Africans and they know it.

There's only so much I can tell the African-British, African-French, or African-Americans; I can't match their passion for original homelands and for ancestral pasts displaced by colonialism or economic desperation.

Since I can't rival Western "African experts" either (despite their long record of getting the continent's problems wrong), who am I left talking to, or on behalf of?

Theoretically, millions of ordinary citizens in Europe and America – more than the population of Africa itself. It is our governments which have imposed the new trading regime upon the developing world. We are so uninformed that we fear to speak. Yet we have voting power. If we exclude ourselves from all dialogues, it is ourselves who can't learn.

Like most of my readers, I can't afford to scoot round Africa on lightning journalistic visits. Instead, I am planning to be the average Northern reader's representative: what can we do, here in our homes, to improve our knowledge and freshen our imaginations?

Unable to write a full political tract, I have raised an African issue in my mind and studied a country where the issue is urgent. My poems then skew off sideways in some unpredictable way. Inevitably, I keep thinking of my own European experience and personal biography, an infection I have tolerated. If charged with narcissism, I'd retort that it's the opposite: a willingness to display how little I know. Talking about politics from supposedly impersonal objectivity means we can be more, rather than less, cruel. My approach is an emotional engagement from the only places emotions come from: our hearts, their *local* history, and our imperfect knowledges.

Only sensational events – famines, wars, Rwandan genocide, or the freeing of South Africa – prompt most Europeans to remember the African nations at all. We can hardly place many of them on the map. It's all "Africa", the imperialist fiction, the hopeless continent.

Liberal writers are too easily scared off by Black Power rhetoric: what the hell business is Africa of ours? None, of course. But Malcolm X said in an interview:

> Whites who are sincere should organise among themselves and figure
> out some strategy to break down the prejudice that exists in white

> communities. This is where they can function more intelligently and more effectively, in the white community itself, and this has never been done.

I don't know about 'never been done', but much of that strategy remains to be created. The former Congo's Patrice Lumumba once snapped that the white man's vision of Africa was one of lion hunts, slave markets, and colonial conquests. Is our modern economic colonialism much better?

Back in the early centuries AD, when Ghana gained control over the mid-Saharan salt mines, its merchants obtained gold from tribes further south by the "dumb barter" method. Tribal miners would leave ore on a river bank; the merchants would leave salt beside it; the tribesmen would return and, if satisfied, take the salt; if not, more salt would have to be added. In this tactful trade there was no cultural interference.

My poems are my Northern salt, left by a common river, only a gesture rather than a barter because obviously insufficient. On my side of the bank they represent a hope that Triad governments will act generously to end the debt spiral and take fuller part in an international programme to revive a continent. Leaving more salt!

Paris, 12 April 1999 / 10 February 2000

14

Our Family Is Full of Problems

A long, easy line of introduction, as if I'm a poet prosing alongside you,
a stranger, half-turning in his enthusiasms. We're in England,
descending the house-combed hillsides of Coventry,
early seventies, when the idea for these poems was born;
and we enter the shattered Hillfields suburb under the ring road.
I show you the surviving top shops,
terraces with wide upper windows blank in dark brick
where once the ribbon weavers' looms throbbed, driven
by a long, easy belt drive through attics of these joined homes
from one combustion engine in the end garden. Came the fall of cotton.
Came Second World War bombs, came socialist planners
bulldozing Hillfields, came the acrid fires of the homeless
on rubbled sites beside high rises which trapped infants
in sweating flats far from their natural earth, families collapsing,
some crime – much exaggerated, some prostitution – from outside.
Came courage to live through a city's class and racial tensions,
scapegoats in 'Coventry's Square Mile of Crime'.
Now came the government again, with a full purse, to restore
the vanished community, as if money could replace the granny in 25
or the old man who played the spoons in 28, or the larger family
that was once the suburb of Hillfields. I turn to you, as if newly excited,
to explain how those planners implanted community centres,
went for mixed housing, sought to make a sunrise in the slums.
And created a middle-class boom instead. See the problem families
scatter as the suburb goes bourgeois. I point to the smart new brick.
See the hard truth of it: a free market nation will stick such families
right at the bottom; they'll never afford a house even one rung
above lowest and slip modestly aside from new building plots
into the next meanest doorway.

This relaxed walking – not a singing – gives us time for specifics;
but to see the problems of families puts a chord string of iron in the heart,
still there many years later in a country obsessed with free markets,
following the gleam of international power blocs, the EU, the WTO.
And I read a *Daily Mail* economist forecasting great wealth
for all free market countries. 'Of course, there will be basket cases,
such as Africa'. And I grab you by the arm.
'Did you hear that? Africa! Not a Coventry suburb, a whole continent
written off in our free trade fanaticism.' As if

holding your arm I face towards Africa and write these poems
as representative of a failed British imagination.

The iron chord is struck and I walk with you in Dar es Salaam.
In golden light move the stereotype dark suits
of World Bankers, planning, funding, organising, implementing,
evaluating corrugated sheets of shanties rattling in the sunny wind.
The government, lenient on forced eviction, has targeted
these slums for upgrading with World Bank funding
still in these early seventies; it will allocate building plots, slap down
fully-serviced cement foundations for squatters, a housing bank for loans,
providing you build to old colonial standards.
Low-income earners, the self-employed, the jobless
can't get these loans, can't build to such standards,
and the Hillfields, Coventry, story repeats itself.
The poor move out to new marginal, unserviced squatterdoms.
I follow them in my imagination and imagine I am following
the old slum-dwellers of Hillfields in Coventry
inexorably moving on.
Come the petit bourgeois, the middle classes,
come the slippery deals in land, till even the Bank admits:
'It is believed that many of the plots have unofficially
transferred to more affluent individuals.'
An inner city opened up to free market forces
will scatter the poor. World trade agreements blindly following
the forces that created a Hillfields are creating an Africa
ever falling behind this financial neo-colonialism,
the World Bank credo, the credo of the GATT, to help an Africa
bulldozed already by its own politicians.
Then I take your arm again and remark, 'I have risked prose,
a walking measure, to explain why I've written these poems.'

Nigeria: Times Primordial

I open Robert Farris Thompson's *Flash of Spirit* and stare at an iron bow, a ritual object for Oshoosi, the archer, brother of the Yoruban iron god, Ogun. Ogun's jurisdiction is wide, extending in Wole Soyinka's plays even to roads and road accidents, where metal is involved.

In Mande creation myth from the Niger River, an ancestral smith descended from heaven early on in the story, just after the ancestral poet-musician did. The smith found drought but when he struck a rock with his iron hammer down came the rain. A Dinka myth from southern Sudan tells how God separated from man when a woman touched God with an iron hoe. As Rousseau believed, the discovery of iron-working marked the crucial step into more advanced civilisation.

The history of early Africa is richer than I can even suggest. But if the gods shoot their bows more swiftly than humans, does a god shoot less or more swiftly with an iron bow than a wooden one? The heavens disdain the cowardly speed of gunfire, with its slow aim and long trajectory.

Oshoosi quickly unleashes his arrow.
We see him only to embrace a shadow.

The Borrowed Bow

The moment stings, shorting like an old wireless
of bakelite body with a trellised raffia screen.
The shadowy corner's acrid with electricity,
blue air frazzed with black
in a cliffside house blank-windowed towards France.
But around the space of shock are other rooms
where old men, sitting by their wirelesses,
wear country check worsteds with a fleck of red
blodged with gravy. This moment
is a vanishing point on a post-war seacoast,
the pier blown up in case of German invasion.

The rooms still have that slow life
moving in them, a termite-gnawed Asante mask
on the walls of a retired colonial official,
an assegai from elsewhere in Africa,
a boot-polish shield, a bow, a poisoned arrow;
for there's an unexplored magic in all time,
a survival even now of a toothless mouth
sopping at a biscuit, a hand trembling
on a bony knee, about to reach
for porcelain on a frame of swivelling trays,
thin finger crooked as for a trigger.

I borrowed the bow of black hardwood,
took it and a bamboo stick into the garden.
Couldn't pull the leather string back;
the magic of the bow-spar wouldn't bend for me.
I knew I was just meddling. So I went indoors
to fiddle with the wireless innards:
electronic emotions and jerky excitements
in the village of valves, which cracked like gunfire,
a tracer arc streaked across dusty connections,
as if before the snap of it, the coil of smoke,
a tiny bow had shot a brilliant arrow.

Coast of Guinea, 1564, Senegambia, 1731

Hakluyt's *Voyages* report how Sir John Hawkins, an Elizabethan captain, slid past the Portuguese warships to conduct hooligan slaving raids upon the Guinea coast. He has moored off the Cape Verde islands on the north-west shoulder of Africa in 1564, and there he is rocking to and fro in his little galleon.

> To speake somewhat of the sundry sortes of these Guyneans; the people of Cape Verde are called Leophares, and counted the goodliest men of all other, saving the Congoes, which do inhabite on this side the cape de Buena Esperança. These Leophares have warres against the Ieloffes, which are borderers by them: their weapons are bowes and arrowes, targets, and short daggers, darts also, but varying from other Negros: for whereas the other use a long dart to fight with in their hands, they cary five or sixe small ones a peece, which they cast with. These men also are more civill then any other, because of their dayly trafficke with the Frenchmen, and are of nature very gentle and loving...

These Africans give meat and drink to a Frenchman shipwrecked on their island in heavy seas. He goes wandering about onshore with a crowd of islanders. With the help of Frenchmen on his own ship, Hawkins slyly woos the man to come on board. Displaying to the Africans how kind he is to their French friend, he hopes to lull the *Leophares* into a false security so as to snatch them up and ship them to the West Indies. But they are warned off by a rival slave ship, the *Minion.*

> ...the 7 of December wee came away, in that pretending to have taken Negros there perforce, the Mynions men gave them there to understand of our comming, and our pretence, wherefore they did avoyde the snares we had layd for them...

Brutal, canny, Hawkins was rarely so thwarted and advanced in social status through his voyages. After his second voyage Queen Elizabeth knighted him and the device on his crest was an African's head and bust with the arms bound.

The lip curls, but how we remember slavery is a matter for care: disgust has slimy entrails of pleasure. The vivid imagination can enter even an evil consciousness, own it briefly, and become readily prurient.

Because the slave trade was vast and records scant, estimates of how many Africans were eventually shipped on the Middle Passage vary between three and twenty million, so obviously no one really knows. Like so much sadism, its details descend to the most scrubby banality: the cramped postures on board the slave ships, head-to-ankles; the actual inches of head-space allowed each captive; the stench; the sordid whippings; the disease; the death rate; the care taken that those not bolted down below deck should be unable to observe how the sails were managed. I'm already sick of recounting it, but the scars on the European soul remain.

Africans and Arabs had a milder version of slavery long before the Portuguese arrival on the continent in the 15th century. But now? You'd think "slavery" would be an utterly dead word, abandoned by our civilisation like the word "apartheid".

The practice survives inside and outside Africa. Lacking any direct knowledge, I read that the slave trade in children continues in West Africa, and that there are delivery routes across the north of the continent and towards the Gulf. An especially vicious trade in women and children seized in southern Sudan has accompanied the civil war there. A UN human rights envoy has charged that Khartoum is not doing enough to remedy the marauding; Khartoum hotly denies this; and a Swiss Christian charity has come under fire for paying to free slaves rescued from northern Sudanese slave masters, since this is said to encourage the trade.

High Priest's Son

The high priest of Bondu
good Muslim told son
take these two slaves
ten day's journey to the English traders
downriver at Joar
in the modern Gambia.
Don't cross river to the Mandingoes
they're too hostile.
River trees curtained
the tall masted slave ship
where Captain Pike was
too mean to strike a bargain.
Son crossed river to the Mandingoes
sold the slaves for cows.
Herding cows along the river
heading back to Bondu
called in for a drink
at a friend's house
hung up gold-hilted
sword gold side-knife
alongside a quiver of arrows
gift of the King of Samba
when a company of Mandingoes
pinioned him and interpreter,
shaved their heads and beards
and changed them into slaves.
Captain Pike bought them
wouldn't wait a fortnight
for the high priest to ransom
trader-slaver son,
now himself a slave.
Captain weighed anchor
for passage to Maryland.

This son since celebrated
as Ayuba Suleiman Diallo
of Bondu sickened
on the Maryland tobacco plantation,
couldn't stand murderous

labour, ran away,
came to the notice of certain
gentlemen for sweetness
of manners and his devotion
to Allah. A letter in Arabic
reached an English philanthropist
who not strong in irony
took pity on a slave of breeding
so Ayuba sailed to England
became a protégé because
of his former station in life,
Job son of Solomon.
Other worthy friends
of the Royal Africa Company
raised subscriptions, bought
Ayuba from slave ship's
proprietor, Mr Hunt,
showed him off at court
sent him back to Bondu
as possible political help
to negotiate routes
to the gold and gum in Bambuk.
The Africa Company failed,
Ayuba last heard of
in company records: a
palaver over two slaves
plus a pawned watch
the company owed him.

Enigma. I lack
evidence: did the
Muslim priest's son
return to his old trade
after such a bitter slavery?

Suez, 1869, 1956

After the Suez Canal opened in 1869, the khedive, Ismail, borrowed so much money to modernise Egypt that he gave his country up to the power of Western bankers. In 1875, the British snapped up the Suez Canal shares for four million pounds. Egypt's financial collapse led to dual Anglo-French "condominium" control over the Egyptian budget and to British military occupation.

By the 1880s and 1890s Britain was concentrating upon two routes to its great prize, India: through Suez and round the Cape. This fixation on the Cape, plus German unification, and preliminary European colonial struggles, combined to step up the incursions into Black Africa. At the 1885 Berlin Conference, the European powers virtually said to each other, 'Grab what you can, as long as we all agree who has what "spheres of influence".' The British premier, Lord Salisbury, sharing out with the French ambassador mountains, rivers, and lakes between the Mediterranean and Lake Chad, reported: 'We have only been hindered by the small impediment that we never knew exactly where those mountains and rivers and lakes were.'

When Nasser nationalised the Canal in 1956, the British entered a war coalition against him but, finally, had to pull their troops out of the Canal zone. The 'Suez War' is called by the Arab world 'The Tripartite Aggression' of Britain, France and Israel.

Political words that mask the causes of their violence: "condominium", "spheres of influence", "small impediment", 'Suez War' – and, even, 'Tripartite Aggression'.

Forearms

A purple-haired woman
with a paper handkerchief for a face
runs down the rue des Messageries.
Between the perspective of buildings
tall crane idle against the lines of morning
and a doleful green lion with navy-blue eyes
tattering down to emerald wraiths
dissipates its body in smoke.
Among the stream of Lubavitchers
this Saturday from the synagogue
floats a half-transparent gesture
with a hand that turns in mid-air
and comes back boldly dark blue.
Feminine ginger forearms
poke from a national marine's white blouse,
black slacks and sailor boy hat,
red-head squatting on the pavement bollard
where rue Faubourg Poissonnières
widens for our supermarket;
could be any teenager's frail life,
enlisted to right our errors
of despair, aggression, superstition.
Cirrus on blue above.
Matt black fighter plane
dropped in the road by a child
sets its heel on the sparkling tarmac,
the silhouette of it skids about and becomes
curling tyre marks, or a relic of
a dangerous attitude, setting childrens' lives
at risk. Our corruption needs copious innocence
to work on: I remember green fields,
a cook crossing to the airmen's mess
at Innsworth, cirrus on blue in that vignette.
They could enlist me then; they couldn't now.
That summer of '57, like a tornado
in my mind I tell you,
green imploding on black
like a green bomb splotch on the Suez Canal.

In this morning's sunshine,
a cook crossing now to the boulangerie
triggered that memory. Opening the *Trib*
two paces down from the Métro,
I see they opened fire on the President of Egypt
yesterday as his motorcade
drove to the Addis Ababa summit.
Nearly caused war with Sudan; young Egyptian
forearms writing out enlistment papers;
one day there's a youth's flayed arm but no youth,
green body tattering down in bomb smoke.

Sudan: 1881 to Modern Times

It will be recalled that the reconquest of the Sudan was initiated by the British Government and that both the Khedive and his ministers, although wishing their lost dominion to be restored, were actually surprised by the decision to advance into Dongola. The Khedive objected on the two grounds that it was merely to assist Italy and that he was not consulted beforehand. His subsequent attitude was that of neutrality and indifference rather than co-operation. As late as April 1898, after the battle of Atbara, Cromer reported that the Khedive had probably no clear ideas of what he wanted either in Egypt or the Sudan, 'but in this particular case he cannot get over the feeling that any advantage now gained in the Sudan constitutes an English rather than an Egyptian success.'

CROMER to SALISBURY, No.57, Secret, 12 April 1898,
P.R.O., F.O. 78/4956, cited by Mekki Shibeika

Today's Sudan has sought to unite the nation under the Maliki version of the Islamic Shari'a laws. Maliki, the majority Muslim sect, is the oldest Sunni legal school; its founder, who died in 795, was an Arab traditionalist for whom jurisprudence should be based on the *Koran* and the Prophet's canonical sayings, the *Hadith*. In Islamic belief Allah is the one truth transcending the material world. For the unperverted intellect this is both obvious and revealed in the sacred texts. Since it's so obvious, everyone in the nation should be subject to the religio-judicial-social structures of that same truth.

For certain Arab nations, Islamic fundamentalism seems a bulwark against Western cultural domination, which is a different intolerance coded into economics and, occasionally, warfare. But the Sudan botched together by Britain a hundred years ago will not fit into an integrationist vision of truth and light. The result has been a world-historical tragedy.

Where the north is Arab, Sudan's south is a mix of Black animist, Christian and left-wing groups. Civil war with the north broke out before independence in 1956, but today's troubles stem from a 1989 coup led by Lt. Gen. Omar Hassan al-Bashir which overturned Sudan's elected civilian government. Abetted by Hassan al-Turabi's harsh National Islamic Front, the regime has restarted the long conflict, a *jihad* in their terms, by attempting to force Islamic law on these non-Muslims.

Some southern rebel leaders – most powerful is the leftist, John Garang – have looked for a new constitution to unify the state. But they have had their own vicious divisions and have practised their own barbarisms. The whole country, with its 100 languages and 40 different cultures, has an uneasy tribal mix. Christianity, for all its humanity, for all its being a persecuted religion, operates as another disruptive politics, another version of paradise. Lonrho has meddled too.

Women and children have been principal victims of a breathtaking callousness. Both sides have blocked humanitarian aid from reaching preventable famines. Rather that hundreds of thousands of villagers should die than that any aid fall into enemy hands or army supply routes be encumbered. Bombings, burnings, looting, torture, assassination, enforced 'conversion to Islam' via starvation, destruction of farming areas, enslavement: these are human rights charges against Khartoum's forces. With truce violations now frequent, new famine threatens this year. Médecins sans Frontières rate the famine in southern Sudan as one of the most underreported stories in the U.S. media, and this is true in the British media, too.

How can one see the end to this suffering? President al-Bashir has recently been talking of permitting the south to secede and this April declared a unliteral ceasefire 'to save the lives and properties of the citizens'. He has apparently distanced himself from the hardest line Islamic faction. Tragically late as it was, run into immediate obstacles as it did, we must hope the wish for ceasefire is sincere. Southern rebels have so far only agreed to extend the uneasy truce.

The moment may be ripe for negotiation and mediation, since Khartoum seems to want better access to the world economy. If so, it must stop being an international pariah. Yet oil and minerals lie – poorly exploited – in the south and the impoverished Islamic north could well do with those resources. It is unclear whether the spectre of a Malikite state integrating north and south will depart so easily, however.

Western diplomacy is working for a solution which allows religious freedom. Britain – ancient begetter of these misshapen national borders – seeks rapprochement with Sudan, but so far unsuccessfully.

I recall wistfully the beautiful spirit expressed by the 'enunciator of gnosis in Islam', Mohyddin ibn Arabi:

> My heart is open to every form: it is a pasture for gazelles [spiritual states], and a cloister for Christian monks, a temple for idols, the kaaba [centre of order] of the pilgrim, the tables of the Torah and the book of the Quran. I practise the religion of Love; in whatsoever direction His caravans advance, the religion of Love shall be my religion and my faith.

Foreigners and Sudan

General Gordon, martyr, can't get in
to wave Victoria's sceptre in the Sudan
created by his death. What was born
from the coupling of North and South –
Africans in the South, Arabs in the North –
he can't cure. A semi-transparent bubble
wall rises to encircle the Sudan, and
he can't get in. Around horizons of sand,
half Europe in extent, the wall-mirage rises
between him and his consequences;
and it's still there, the wall-mirage,
leaving his ghost-image on the outside.

Gordon should have been the tall movie actor
from our own day, posing, noble and careless,
white-uniformed on the palace staircase
before the bright-blooded swords of the Mahdi
(the truly-guided one of Mohammed).
But the real pint-sized Scot, blue-eyed,
fearless, fanatic, heroic-minded –
a British Turko-Egyptian governor-mercenary
following Cairo's policy of conquest –
becomes in our mind's ghostliness
huge and demonic in travelling lights
round and round this immense wall.

In the North, tolerant Islam or purified;
in the South, Christian tribes or terrified:
monolithic state, or separatist,
Shari'a's law or outlawed communist;
famine, massacre, torture, mutilation,
two million dead in a modern nation.
And Gordon's image, like a mime feeling
an invisible window, goes dancing
in agony round the vast circumference
while the rest of history unrolls along the Nile
inside the semi-transparent wall; so
he can't get in, into the Sudan.

Alive, he was that pseudo governor-general
(that real figure posing inside the wall)
a governor-general ornate in the uniform
he himself designed. Or at his martyrdom
in the white uniform, speared many times,
somewhat a movie actor after all,
tumbling down the palace steps of Khartoum,
decapitated, against the Mahdi's wishes:
oh, this would be a different tale told by dervishes.
'Stop it,' mouths the mime, seeing himself fall,
and dances round outside the wall.

Behind those rainbow surfaces all fades
into pastel colours, as if cruelty were walled in
by bubble shine when the eye grows fearful.
It's not just Gordon: we ourselves can't get in.
The eyes of strangers are filmed with dust,
a fly crawling, starved head turned aside.
Now we know what Gordon never knew.
Outside, we clutch our money with cheque-
stubby fingers, and have the easy distrust
of non-belief. Yet we're old Gordon's ghost,
still mercenary: we dance around the wall
that separates us from our consequences:

'Don't let these foreign people fall,' we say,
'Don't let them fall.'

Ethiopia: Modern Times

Down the Nile, across the savannah, the Sahelian and desert areas in the north of West African countries, back towards Chad, over to Djibouti and Somalia in the east, Islam holds its sway. Here at home, on the Paris Métro, I see the orderly, affectionate Muslim families from Senegal, Gambia, Mali or Niger, the white caps and long robes; and, though I shall never relinquish dislike of female submission, I know I may not penetrate their privacy.

These encounters mean that even before I begin the journey south of the Sahara, it's the women of Africa that come to mind. In the big African cities, in radical politics, in the intellectual worlds, feminism is making its slow, slow way. In the countrysides, whether Christian, Islamic, animist or agnostic, traditional societies are shielded from change by poverty and isolation. There, in some small village in Togo or Ethiopia, the women still bind the community together by unremitting work.

Ethiopia and Eritrea have this year renewed their terrible border warfare. Yet, as in Paris, so it is across the wild spread of Africa: we may not intrude into family life. Within the most severe hardship, or as the desert creeps down, or under the most corrupt and authoritarian regimes, peoples are always living their own lives of intense preoccupation.

A Woman in Ethiopia

Through the telescope's smoking lens
I see a woman rising in her heat of limbs
from the red desert of Ethiopia;
a priest above her holds a cross
and reads from a dark book: she doesn't
think of me though I think of her intently
and watch the bitter smoke of her sweet fires
making haze round a claystack chimney lodged
in thatch on her circular house of stones.

I speak her country's name but my blazed trail
gives out in this interior. The woman's mood
remains mysterious as she rises. If it's joy,
it has nothing to say but 'Join us'; but I can't
walk beside her child (wearing a Baltimore
Orioles 'cheater) across old battlegrounds
to the well. He secretes a social closeness
born in the swift mood below the rib-cage,
behind the forehead, under the swollen belly.

Often the insubstantial passing thing
counts – myself at a dance passing by my former
lover's dress now topped by a baseball jacket –
deserts spread in certain of my memories,
trivial compared with these red hills of Ethiopia
eroded by farm failures of the dispossessed,
coniferous forest of zigba and tid, disappeared,
coffee bush brittle twigged, cattle bony
on the shoulder, malaria in the lower plains.

I've spoken the country, can't count its secret joy,
interior of stones mottled with cooking tar,
misted by cobwebs, a woman rising
in her heat, walking towards the inner place
of celebration, the wrested feet of a pullet
no longer dusty, bones thrown into leaden water,
some joyful mood my melancholy can't infect;
there's bubbling within the door shadows,
for the unnamed occasion. Shame's my borderline,

since, however far I go, I won't get hungrier,
and poverty has stages I shall never know.
They tie the gut in ivory knots; a little boy
can only waddle with his belly or a girl
lying in mama's arms hurl all her heart
into her yelling. The tourists curve out of these
deserts and emerge on blinding shores,
where eyesight swivels, dragging sheets of light
too sparkling to match our own dull hearts to.

A woman rises from a stool this morning/night.

The Sahel: Present Day

There is, in most poor countries, a sophisticated awareness of the kind of agricultural practices that are sustainable. In India, China, Indonesia and also in many parts of Africa, there are, in peasant farming communities, traditions of terracing, crop rotation, natural fertilisers and animal husbandry that long predate the arrival of European technology. But poor countries often find themselves trapped in a downward spiral in which the combined pressures of poverty and rising population lead to sound practices being abandoned.

SHRIDATH RAMPHAL, quoted in Stewart Boyle & John Ardill, *The Greenhouse Effect* (London: New English Library, 1989).

When sound agricultural practices are abandoned in rich countries, the excuses, therefore, undergo a change in tone.

Soot

A whole nation driving into a sooty cloud
can't see how a demand for comfort
creates a wind strong enough to rip
the black soil off from Fenland
and hang it up against the smoky sunshine,
while government says, 'Drive through that:
and we'll all be wealthy one day!'
Once, the sea draining from those acres
left Britain this rich harvesting. But us,
we're car-owners travelling blind
through farmlands of hedgeless fields
which hunger for high yields.
You know, when topsoil goes for good
there's nothing underneath but stodgy clay;
The clay is surfacing across England
it plates with grey the black flatlands formerly
pinstriped with vivid greens of potato tops
drained by dykes like silver wires.

Blinded.

Dunes are on the move in Western Africa.
The dunes are moving in on Nouakchott,
four miles a year, reaching outskirts
where refugees form squatter camps.
Burkina Faso's camels
heaved over on the roadside like lorries in ditches.
Mali, Nigeria, Niger, Northern Ghana,
Lake Chad six per cent the size it used to be,
people tempted into apathy,
their goats are wandering in the desert.
Africans enriched by independence
now, like colonialists, in ugly parodies
of tribal land-grabbing, oust farmers
who walk blinded into clouds of dust.
The same farmers, urged by necessities,
drive nomads ever further inland
across the desert margin, the Sahel.
Red Saharan dust over Europe gathering,

turning into soot.

34

Zimbabwe and the Missionaries: 19th Century

After Shaka had begun to make the Zulus feared throughout southern Africa, Mzilikazi, a royal son of the Khumalo, took his tribe to become vassals in Shaka's army. They learnt the new discipline of close quarter fighting with short stabbing assegais behind long oxhide shields. Even as Shaka was creating the Kwa Zulu nation, Mzilikazi broke with his chief and led the Khumalo north to build a large kraal named Ekuphumuleni, the Place of Rest; he constructed fortified kraals for a growing army composed of his own tribe and those he had conquered in his brutal journey.

His tribe retained Shaka's fighting methods, and so this enlarged Khumalo tribe became known as the Matabele, probably meaning 'those who disappear behind their shields'.

But this Place of Rest was set in parched land; also, Shaka's arm could reach that far. Mzilikazi went north some more; and then, to flee the Boers trekking up from the Cape region, north yet again, arriving in present-day Matabeleland about 1840. Nowadays, it is part of Zimbabwe.

Mzilikazi had a friend, a formidable missionary, the Rev. Robert Moffat. When Mzilikazi arrived in Matabeleland, Moffat went to see him there in 1854, and established a London Missionary Society station in the king's terrain five years later. The Matabele were notorious for fierceness, but during Moffat's stay in his kingdom, Mzilikazi was known to deal leniently with offenders he would otherwise have executed, because his friend did not like the shedding of blood.

> Mzilikazi loved the Reverend Robert Moffat:
> he'd lean on his shoulder and say
> 'My heart's all white as milk, for you've shown kindness
> to my indunas; I ordered them to find me
> a missionary and they'd have died
> at my hand if they'd failed;
> yet you, a stranger, knowing this,
> fed them and came to my kraal.
> In so far as you did this to them you did it to me
> and you have carried me in your arms.'
>
> Because of this cleanness in an ancient heart,
> both gentle and murderous,
> Moffat heard his own Christ's words
> spoken by the Bull Elephant of the Matabele.

Robert Moffat had a son, a missionary, John. Mzilikazi had a son, a king, Lobengula. And now we have a different story.

The King's Garden

In old Bulawayo was a king's garden –
Lobengula's, son of Mzilikazi
who came from forests of Ngome
and founded the Matabele people.
Some garden!
A bamboo stockade floored with maggoty dung
grazed by hundreds of sheep and goats.
Lobengula sat on a block of wood,
a huge man, smiling, worried, friendly,
cruel in the laws of the tribe.
Around him 30 whites, wanting to mine
legendary gold, scrabbling for treaties,
mistranslated for the illiterate king
by the smooth missionary Helm
whom Cecil Rhodes was paying well.
Three other envoys of Rhodes
squatted on haunches in the dung.
The dapper London lawyer Maguire,
MP, Fellow of All Souls, stuck
out a leg to raise his buttocks from the mire.
A chorus greeted this discourtesy.
'Gh-h-o,' called the younger warriors gleefully,
'He wants to be as big as the king.'
The king of the Matabele,
Lobengula, sat on his wood block, smiling.

An official from the Rhodes mines
in Kimberley, one Thompson,
muttered aside to Maguire: 'It's as much
as your life's worth to shirk homage.'
Down squatted Maguire, back into dung,
down squatted Charles Dunnel Rudd,
and it was managed like that,
the Rudd Concession,
born in the filth of false homage.
The king's most trusted white friend,
a son of the great missionary Moffat,
spoke in his ear (but secretly for Rhodes).

The king, tricked about the treaty's words,
and thinking of a few small mining holes,
signed away his country.
Better advised, he panicked, sent
envoys to the white Queen, proclaiming
'Lobengula did not say these words'
(for land couldn't be owned in private).
Unthinkable to the king a queen could lie.
Victoria wrote a warning letter
in the Africans-speak-English language:
'A King gives a stranger an ox,
not his whole herd –
beware in placing your trust.'
Her messenger, Maund, in league with Rhodes,
quietly lost this letter,
and men in high places
returned the envoys roundabout
to the king via South America,
while Rhodes finagled his Royal Charter,
an excuse for the Charter Ro law
of the sjambok and of the Maxim gun
mounted within the king's kraal,
its tripod spiked into the dung.
Yes, it was managed like that,
an excuse for wholesale invasion,
seizure of the king's maggoty garden,
slaughter of the Matabele peoples
as they fled the Bulawayo kraal.
And there was hardly any gold.
The treaty men simply settled the land.

We British of a third generation
have seen this treachery playing out
down dishonourable decades, until –
Matabele and Mashona fighting back –
colonials retired, disgruntled,
to our childhood suburb. Sometimes
a garden we stopped at:
quite manic with
its lawn of absolute green. Triangles
and crescents for flower beds held

brick-orange lumps of marigolds
and bruised-yellow pansies in military lines,
an exact border of daffodils,
blooded by tulips, green budding red,
like laughter turned tubercular.
The ancient captain behind panes of glass
in clover-shaped concrete mouldings
glowered as we wondered why
his mind delighted in these rows of bulls' eyes,
grass edges moustache-clipped,
beauty so tight-chested
that it gave a harsh cough,
opened its windows at us,
and ordered small boys to clear off,
go to the cliffs, get away from the iron gate.

Malawi: First World War

A squad of white colonist forces advances, an accurate rifle raps out, a Maxim gun chatters, a tribesman falls clutching an antiquated, malfunctioning firearm or just a spear. In Hollywood SciFi, the tribesman would be the valiant Earthman struggling against extra-terrestrial invaders whose weaponry has undreamt-of power. Until quite recently in white history writing, the heroes of this scenario have been the extra-terrestrials, ourselves.

African historians have at last made us look at the falling tribesman. In the 19th century, resistance to colonialism could be large-scale – the Asante's decades of battle against the British, and the Mahdist rebellions (northern Sudan, Somalia); medium-scale – Samori Ture against the French in southern Sudan, the British crushing the Ijebu in southern Nigeria, and Kabarega's anti-British guerrilla warfare in Uganda; or small-scale and therefore particularly courageous – the 300 partisans mobilised by Diop against the French in the Senegambia.

In Matabeleland, the dying King Lobengula bequeathed to his followers a struggle to restore the monarchy. The resulting Matabele and Mashona rebellion of the 1890s was only surpassed in danger for a colonial regime by the Maji Maji revolt which had devastated the entire south of German East Africa by 1907: after brutal repression, between 250,000 and 300,000 Africans were dead from bullets or starvation. In barren Southwest Africa, the Germans nearly annihilated the Herero cattle herders.

As the First World War begins to end German prospects in Africa, I am haunted by the image of a Nyasaland preacher from that time; he's wearing a pyjama jacket under his coat and running for his life. I am haunted, too, by hopes for modern Malawi, struggling back to democracy after the dictatorship of Hastings Banda which left the country burdened with debt. And so, with all deference and for Westerners who won't read it elsewhere, I recount one of that country's founding legends.

A Salvo for Malawi

Chotsa chipewa! Choka!
Take off your hat to me! Now scram!

Say you've never heard of John Chilembwe,
or of his mission church at Mbombwe
HQ for his First War Rising
first salvo for the Malawi nation.
Yet as surely as my mother lived
on the tracer-path planet
left behind in our world's world line
so surely my memory discovers her
not in chemical coding but alive there still
and so surely John Chilembwe still gives off
that black light in his black preacher's suit
or is alive in all our pasts before our birth
not in the photos recovered when they shot him down
but still running from the troops
towards Mozambique unarmed, hot-fleshed,
in dark blue coat, striped pyjama jacket
coloured shirt, grey flannel trousers
running for about a mile before
Mlanje Police Private Naluso shot him;
the bullet spun him around and around,
Sergeant Useni hit him again,
I hit him through the head,
said Garnet Kaduya, Church of Scotland,
in a language truly dead, but Chilembwe was
spinning
as they pulled and snapped the life-thread
in that present moment.
He's still alive as he turns
just a second before the shooting;
and so I may tell you his story,
not tapping into memory but into time,
and refire the first salvo for the end
of white hegemony in Central Africa.

You must come along. Whether you're a
Caribbean in Brixton able to instruct me,
or white middle-class in Surrey,

or an elderly person on welfare in Consett,
or a blurty-eyed young person,
whether you ever read poetry or not,
all our paradoxes meet in Chilembwe's life.

Let me take you into the stolen land
by the huge lake, and I'll come to greet you
as some District Commissioner
my tie round its stiff collar
like a ribbon round a white plastic pot
from your own days. I'm still alive
in arm-creased jacket parted
over tweaked waistcoat,
topi going grey, white ducks
flattened on my shins. You
come back to me with old books:
I come towards you with your modern
news cuttings: racial attacks in England
and Wales doubled in five years,
firebombings, knife attacks, killings.
'Many black Britons
might eagerly return to their countries.'
And we meet on a bush track
marked with stone spikes.
I doff my hat to the future
as the natives doff their hats to me
even at a thousand yards' distance.

The Shire Highlands are ours by treaty
stolen from Nyasa tribes illiterate
in our law: price, a gun,
some calico, two red caps, other things,
at one-tenth of a penny per acre
plus road-making, mining rights.
Doubled hut taxes make them work
on white farms, like the harsh Bruce estate
run by Livingstone's distant descendants;
planters whip them for misdemeanours,
their goats and chickens grabbed,
no pay, or money thrown on the ground.
Sheer need drives them
to recruit in our German war,
the Boche attacking by lake and land

from the North, long lines of porters
carrying munitions on their heads,
dying in a two-thirds majority
over the whites, their only democracy.
It's unjust, but they're not ready for any other.
As Miss Marguerite Roby said in her recent book:
'It is conceivable that the coloured man in Central Africa
would be happier if left entirely to himself;
but the march of progress is not to be arrested
and when the conquering white enters a black country
labour he must and will have,
let the theorists rave as they will.'

Chiradzulu, you say from your future.
Is this the site of the rising? Where was the church?

You're talking of John Chilembwe.
I know John, mission educated,
secretive Baptist type in dark suits,
complains we've led his people
to war against the Germans.
He's probably infected with Ethiopianism,
a dangerous millennarian creed.
Who knows what he preaches in that church of his?
Africa for the Africans, I suppose.

Ethiopianism? you say from your future,
I thought that was Marcus Garvey,
rephrased by the Rastafarians.

Marcus who? I'm quoting the 68th psalm,
'Ethiopia shall soon stretch out her hands to God.'
You see the brick-built church
rising before us over by Mbombwe, roofs
frosted with photographic light? Its towers
make it a unit of measurement
fit for your Bromley road but here lost
in the Nyasaland bush.
They've laid in the mortar crudely,
harsh lines stripe the entrance steps,
and like a double-exposure the broad white hat
of its pastor, his furiously serious face, drab suit,
almost appear for us in the archway.

That's John Chilembwe:
he seems to absorb all the light.

But, you say from your future,
he was shot on a hillside
after his followers had removed the head
from William Jervis Livingstone
the Bruce estate manager
and stuck it up in this very church.

Your future events rush towards me in a herd.
The missionaries began the trouble,
Watchtower people,
Seventh Day Adventists,
Seventh Day Baptists, one called Booth
took Chilembwe on as a servant,
sent him to America to mix
with the radicals there.
John came back as a qualified reverend
to set up African-run missions
with American Negro support.
Had the effrontery to build this huge church
and prayer houses across the Bruce estate,
which Livingstone had to burn
or the natives would think they had land rights.
But all was manageable until the war.
Here is part of a letter
we censored from the *Nyasaland Times*
under emergency regulations.

THE VOICE OF AFRICAN NATIVES IN THE PRESENT WAR

We understand that we have been invited to shed our innocent blood
in this world's war which is now in progress throughout the wide
world...

A number of our people have already shed their blood, while
some are crippled for life. And an open declaration has been issued.
A number of Police are marching in various villages persuading
well built natives to join in the war. The masses of our people are
ready to put on uniforms ignorant of what they have to face or why
they have to face it...

Because we are imposed upon more than any other nationality
under the sun. Any true gentleman who will read this without the
eye of prejudice will agree and recognise the fact that the natives
have been loyal since the commencement of this Government, and

that in all departments of Nyasaland their welfare has been incomplete without us. And no time have we been ever known to betray any trust, national or otherwise, confided to us. Everybody knows that the natives have been loyal to all Nyasaland interest and Nyasaland institutions. For our part we have never allowed the Nyasaland flag to touch the ground, while honour and credit have often gone to others. We have unreservedly stepped to the firing line in every conflict and played a patriot's part with the Spirit of true gallantry. But in time of peace the Government failed to help the underdog. In time of peace everything for Europeans only. And instead of honour we suffer humiliation with names contemptible. But in time of war it has been found that we are needed to shed our blood in equality. It is true that we have no voice in this Government. It is even true that there is a spot of our blood in the cross of the Nyasaland Government...

JOHN CHILEMBWE
In behalf of his countrymen.

Your future rushing... tells me
that this man is more dangerous
than we'd thought. Time is flickering...
Something's happening here...
as we stand on this bush path together...
how has the time passed by...?
Well, I have been badly shocked by recent events.
Shall I tell you how his so-called battalions,
no more than two hundred natives,
killed Mr Livingstone a few weeks ago?
It's an exciting story:
The whites were making merry
at the Blantyre Sports Club.
The natives with their spears and an axe
went creeping across the Bruce estate in the night,
haunting the Livingstone house.
Mrs MacDonald, undressed,
opened a bathroom window,
saw shadowy Africans holding sticks.
Thought the sticks were firewood, d'you see.
Livingstone himself was letting a cat out
when five or six natives broke in with spears,
and he fought them with rifle butt
from room to room until they stabbed him.
Mrs Livingstone told me:
'He did not appear to be dead.

He fell on his side.
I tried to turn him over on his back but did not succeed.
I looked for a bottle of Port wine.
The bottle was snatched out of my hand by a native
and just then another…came in with an axe
and proceeded to cut off my husband's head…in my presence.'
Two other Europeans were murdered and –

I've heard enough, you say from your future,
of the deaths of three whites
in one murderous gesture I may not condone.
You forget the Africans sagging into the dust,
their whole continent now unremembered by Britons
who still profit from Northern hegemony,
whose shiny liberal shoes walk over these memories.
But where was Chilembwe?

Back in his church, waiting for the head,
or upon Chilimangwanje Hill,
praying on his Mount of Olives.
He intended martyrdom, not victory:
'Strike one blow and then we die.'
We chased him across another hillside,
his Calvary,
recovered a pair of gold spectacles
and a pair of pince-nez, the right lens
missing in each case,
found next to his half-starved body.
Then we obliterated his memory
and dynamited his church. If you look again
across the bush you'll see
the great church first bowed to its knees
like a shot giraffe, then the roof
sagging in like tarmac in an earthquake.
And we have imprisoned those Adventist missionaries
beside the African traitors
because the white fanatics set the fuse
and won't be executed for it.
D'you know what they say?
'Six more of our teachers have been taken prisoner.
The flogging of prisoners goes on just the same.
I do think they might have some consideration for us
and punish them outside the place. A European

ought not to be allowed to stay in a place like this.
Sunday of all days is the worst.'

Jehovah's fanatics fomenting
new troubles in the Thirties –
is that, you say from your future,
why Malawi banned
Watchtower Witnesses with their wild
and democratic armageddons?

Where's Malawi?
The question returns me
to a modern time of writing.
In my mind this past survives
as a more-than-memory.
Not even Chilembwe's religious myths
pass away, though in my own beliefs
no man was resurrected
after any Calvary except in the strange survivals
of all this time as a haunting
of our sadly avaricious, racist British lives,
survivals as shadows outside a cosy house
where we sit eating goats and chickens
grabbed from Africa via foreign loans,
money thrown on the ground.

Chilembwe said:

> I am afraid of the war, which exists between Great Britain and
> Germany, war the results of which are world wide, and which has
> already paralysed all business in Africa. I don't know how you can
> help us, but by all means try to send us something to sustain our
> lives and bodies, for we, as well as those who are taking part are
> greatly in need. Please in some way send us help, or leave us to die
> if you choose. At this writing I am penniless. Pray that God in his
> Chariot may bring messengers of peace and that the Nations may
> be brought back to the Temple of Peace.

And we imagine the First World War is over!
'...kindhearted Chilembwe,
who wept with and for the writer's
fever-stricken and apparently dying child,'
wrote the restless Seventh Day man, Joseph Booth.

Kenya and the Mau Mau: 1950

Round about 1950, my older school friends in Bournemouth suddenly grew up and became National Servicemen off to fight the Mau Mau in Kenya.

Thinking of this in bed this morning, I sleepily recall, for no apparent reason, a balcony overlooking a high-roofed shopping arcade in my Bournemouth suburb of Boscombe. Up there, a thin woman in black tulle is vamping at an echoey piano and, below, I am staring at a model plane in a toyshop window.

Instantly, I have a waking dream of the map of Africa covered with newsprint-sized words. Words and map appear all-at-once under my eyelids. Glimpsed from my eye-corners, the phrases seem like surrealist automatic writing: Freudian misspellings, half meanings, puns, strange word combinations – a frequent kind of word-vision that I have now that I use computers so much. The moment I try to capture a word in sight it changes. Even individual letters instantly change into other letters when I look at them on the mental screen. But by a psychological trick of not attending, I can let a brief word-chain float sidelong into conscious memory like a wisp of cloud.

I retrieve the words, 'jusu christi areobuzzer'. 'Areobuzzer' seems a misspelling for *aerobuzzer*, my childhood name for paper aeroplanes. Flicking my attention on to 'jusu' made the word change to 'juju', as if Christ on the aeroplane of his cross had transformed into African magic.

The Childhood Map

An Africa the size of a British park
cracked like a white map,
a manageable terrain,
or coloured in with adventures
for boyhood dreams of the bush,
brown and sere, gazelles,
scouted by cheetahs on their hills,
streaming over the high plateaux
of Kenya beneath the fuselage
of a plane that lands long ago, lightly,
into history. In present time
it could only land tourists,
and it's worse than that.

Locust aircraft turns on its wire arm
lands in a toyshop window. Trembles.
Child minds excited but blank.
As adults, we are reading
liberal history books:
the oily tones of the Whitehall elite
with their city interests and ties
setting up Kikuyu Home Guards
to fight Kikuyu Mau Mau.
For every white man killed
four hundred Africans killed.

Toy planes still landing long ago.
Kenya gripped by one-party rule now
its opposition enfeebled.
If Britain were beset by famines,
would it be governable?
Shining pupils of our aristocratic schools
rise to well-fed pomposity
of managing nations
of making the EU competitive
against boys running ragged
down river banks in Nairobi.

The toyshop window lights up again.
A slender plane with medicaments
or is it a white human body
is flying low over Africa dispensing
a fraction of western money spent on AIDS:
HIV truck drivers in Rwanda
say, 51 percent; Uganda
36 percent; Kenya who
knows, 19 percent; commercial
sex workers in bars
34 to 88 percent –

the stanza
breaks apart, Africa
cracks like a painted tin landscape
in a child's small attention.
Elsewhere beyond this window
its greatness breathes like a leopard.
Will these statistics never be finished?
Can we never get on the right side of them?
Watching our little plane
on its slender piece of wire
land behind the window.

Kenya: Wild Life

In Livingstone's last journals – where his men carried him, exhausted and haemorrhaging, through the marshes of Bangweolo – he writes:

> A blanket is scarcely needed till the early hours of the morning, and here, after the turtle doves and cocks give out their warning calls to the watchful, the fish-eagle lifts up his remarkable voice. It is pitched in a high falsetto key, very loud, and seems as if he were calling to some one in the other world. Once heard, his weird unearthly voice can never be forgotten – it sticks to one through life.

In the 1880 edition this is accompanied by an attractive engraving of a fish eagle screeching its strange call as it surveys a lake from a wooden hippopotamus trap; it looks for all the world like an osprey I remember seeing in Wales.

Ospreys… there are birds which are clarion to us, as in the Kenyan poet Marjorie Oludhe Macgoye's great lament for modern Kenya, spoken by the legendary Mathenge, the only Mau Mau general to be missing after the war, who tells us that he once advanced with bugles as loud as the ndete bird.

In New York one day, I heard the fish eagle's voice coming from the speaker of a tape recorder.

The Birds of Kenya

I *Our Generation*
(for Steve Carey)

I hear the birds of Kenya singing as I write this
for Steve Carey who liked recorded birdsong
as I do, the cassette shrill, a door falling-to
on squeaky hinges. Steve: a grating laugh
of one who was buff-crested, sulphur chested,
lost like me in distant islands of sound
in sonophilia for Kenyas and Britains and native
American wood, with its double-toned wood thrush.
Our own generation at its song.
Calls of 'Will be!', 'Will be!', like a Wilbye
madrigal, every generation in hope
of its many-coloured men and women.
And the fish eagle's magical feet snatch silver fish
from gold-breeding lakes at all dawns,
as we snatch syllables from standstill moments
and lift that sound, a moment isolated, into sunlight.

White-bellied go-away birds flock from trees
whenever a nation is betrayed by another;
grey-capped warblers duetting on the boughs
of Kenya for every heart that nations ever broke
in a world arena of forest with big cats growling
and a concert of birds in the leafy auditorium,
gutturals from the syrinx and whistling from the beak,
perspectives of their calls in forest architectures.

Tone deaf, all these birds; don't do the sol-fa,
neither did the priestly herons of Dylan Thomas
nor the ndete bird of Marjorie Oludhe Macgoye.
One totem tree is lightning-struck, over by the lake,
mosquitoes tightly whining on the dusty surface
like skipped musical notes circling in minute annotation
above the matte black water of the wordless
right to natural prey, even the fish mouthing it.

A bird of predator-oracle, the Kenyan fish eagle,
grips the heartwood of the stricken tree, its calls
like the cackle of a gull and the hooing of an owl,
eagle notes of pure cruelty, whose suspense
glides briefly, simply necessary, over its own waters.
And I remember the Welsh osprey has the same feet
pinning the heart-broken syllable to the branch,
beak drawing out cords from ragged brown innards.

Seeing through Blindness: Modern Times

Craftier Westerners than me may learn to imitate the conversation of Africans themselves as they talk about the continent: very hip. Then you can appear expertly liberal and enlightened, despite your car, your middle-class lodgings in London, New York or Paris. But our Western lives show that we are not enlightened, that we'd hate it if the developing world threatened our standard of living. Our false consciousness dulls our mind-sight and we drift into complacency.

I read as much literature in English by African authors as I can get hold of. The tone is quite different from the disguised superiority of Western journalism with its predilection for horrors-at-a-distance.

In African authors the depth of a culture comes across, or a striking emotional honesty, or a sharpness of political analysis that leaves Western cynicism behind; and we find humour, like that in Congolese music, or, again, stalwart women and men confronting their poverty, the breakdown of their society, and international white prejudice. We are set into the life of a poor village and we see the warmth there, the inventive variety of second-hand clothing, the constant making-do with odds and ends, the fact that hope-lessness, undesirable as it may be, has another aspect which is metaphysical: timeless patience.

If only I could breathe into my poems that other, greater spirit of Africa. But there, when the call comes to be positive, my cultural distance is most a barrier. For Western writers, the darker tones are easier to hit because faults are easier to describe than that kind of virtue which comes from the whole person.

I reach for a tape of African music and catch a rhythm from it.

The Unseeing Drum

If I drummed on the long Dahomey tambour,
I'd be bumbling, blind in ludicrous Western clothes,
that tambour's wooden tubes stepped at the foot
like a half-closed sea captain's telescope; I'd be

drumming of old things I can half-see: of bamboo-
stilted houses elongated by water reflections
as if I were paddling to the floating market of Ganvié
while fishermen cast nets in jelly-fish patterns.

So, almost, I drum on the Dahomey tambour.
My hands can't make me see, and I haven't looked
at Mali's thatched houses, the mud rain-washed off
walls ribbed by uncooked bricks poking through.

Or I put Zairean-style Soukous music into my ears
and watch pesticide machines huff injections
into a Kinshasa sewer; a woman's hut in Topoke holds
two bamboo beds, food bowls on a stick-legged shelf.

Tapping blindly in rhythm on my work-table,
I see women across Africa stoop to chipped bowls
of peanuts and they grunt at their labour, the body rocking,
scale-arm burdened by the cupped hand's loveliness.

With my hands tapping perhaps without sanctity
as on taut antelope skin, I glimpse wooden shanties
in Nouakchott, corridors of all doors, black-
swathed mothers holding babies with two hair clumps

on their shaven heads, one at the front, one at the back.
Unseeing, I must yet see, boat-making in Niger
where a steel bar burns holes in wood slabs and the thin
pirogue spreads out like crocodile-chewed nougat.

The women are off to market, millet stalks on oxen:
swaggering on camels is reserved for the men.
The children scoop pits in sand, playing Marella
– or tic-tac-toe. Half-blinded by the male sun,

the boys dream of being horsemen. In Uganda
other children learn shopping, sugar cane, gourds,
for merchandise; muzzled camels gloom by a sidewalk
hat souk in Libya, coned pots with cockerel tails.

Structural beams spike from baked earth mosques
in Burkina Faso, a palm trunk with flute-holes makes
a village ladder, woman climbing, hand reaching
for grain and fruit to dry on the roof of her house.

Skate fish flap down into Sahel sand, gasp,
and become dark tents; a Guinea woman's hair
is the shape of a seal's head; by the gushing springs
of Chaouen black robes float over sparkling cobblestones.

Elsewhere, money and talent whisper their telepathy
in coastal capitals, yet everywhere as names flash by
in my drumming women appear, washing clothes
under river bridges, *un amour* shadowed on the bankside.

Sunlight glares down those city avenues where blurred
humans hurry into their potential for richness:
in Conakry, pineapples enter a factory chunker;
Moroccan biologists work in impossible snowfalls

of cotton branches to improve yields; alluvial gold
is panned in Ilesha; a hand pours libations
into chemical pipettes in Lagos; it was Barclays put
an ugly wafer-biscuit bank on those oily streets.

White blocks front the Zanzibar straits of Tanzania,
where the canoe's striped sail bounds out on its ropes,
fishing boats tug at the men launching them,
hulls leap in surf, and the flying water is the pleasure.

I ask you, 'Pretend to have sight a moment, for the sun
under our lids will warm us.' A real blind drummer
from the animist Dogon in Mali, taps on the skin
with curved stick, seeing all that I don't see, and I see him.

Somalia: Traditional Practices

I turn into a shabby street in Paris's 11th arrondissement. Galvanised sheeting clads the wire fences that surround vacant lots left by urban blight. A single line of window-blown buildings with walls of red brick or flaking plaster has a street door with a label slapped on: 'Maison des femmes'. Inside, a sociologist leads me past classroom desks and sits me down on an uncomfortable settee. She tells me how the Groupe de Femmes pour l'Abolition des Mutilations Sexuelles (GAMS) tries to educate female African immigrants in Paris about cliterodectomy and more severe forms of infibulation.

Some 100 million girls are said to undergo circumcision in more than 20 countries on the African continent. Genital mutilation is often practised, usually on young children, by traditional circumcisors in illiterate rural areas, using razor, knife or sharp object. In the mildest form, all or part of the clitoris is removed; in the severest, or Pharaonic, the clitoris and both the labia minora and majora are excised and the wound sewn up, sometimes using thorns; a reed, tube, or matchstick is inserted to leave a small passage for urine and menstrual blood. An intermediate process leaves a larger opening and more of the genitalia intact. The details vary: sometimes the children "celebrate" their rite of passage, for example by dancing; other times, no elaborate ceremony is staged as among Somalian nomads.

A GAMS team of French women, mostly doctors and African women of various occupations, work in baby clinics advising immigrant mothers how to bring up children in a foreign culture. Three-quarters of these mothers are of Soninke stock from the Senegal River region – the old French West Africa. Tact is everything: where names indicate an ethnic group practising girl-child circumcision, the GAMS worker still waits to be asked about it.

The operation is not only illegal in France and exquisitely painful; it is also medically dangerous. It can involve: infection of vulva or urinary areas, gynaecological problems and septicemias which can lead to death, possible sterility, difficult and complicated childbirth with risk of tearing the perineum, plus the wounding or elimination of the female organ of sexual pleasure leading to a lessening or disappearance of feeling and to sexual dissatisfaction. Mental health repercussions may include anxiety, anguish, depression, even suicide.

Since I wrote this, the self-declared independent Republic of Somaliland, whose capital is Hargeisa in the north-west, has been trying to eradicate female circumcision by 2000 and UNICEF is backing them. Senegal has in January 1999 joined the countries which have outlawed the practice, although with more than a million people thus facing jail, it is not clear how the law can be enforced. In France, an infibulation victim's complaint led to a highly-publicised prosecution of the "cutter" and her circle of mothers.

But I have reached the limit of my poetry: Western people's ignorance of traditionalist societies is too profound. Like Alice Walker and Pratibha Parmar working in West Africa, you could make a courageous film on the subject. Failing that, a poem might yet become a sort of film shot from a distance, an attempt to project on to the air, via a beam of good wishes, an imagined ceremony for the sake of young girls who are infibulated without ceremony by nomad Somalians, almost on the move.

The Infibulation Ceremony

A Jeep, its shock absorbers gone, thumps
across pocks in the level desert scrub
faster than the black-faced sheep with fat tails
prodded onwards by the nomad women.

If we have time and water
we stop and let the clan drink;
if we have neither we drive on
inventing our film about infibulation.

We drive up to a low escarpment
and look down on a hollow littered with people,
livestock scattered among the rocky slopes
by a well cairned with boulders.

Near this home well on their April journey
the women dismantle the hut sticks
from the ship slew of camel humps,
setting up Nissen huts of mats and skins.

Herded then by a man, disburdened
camels sigh and settle down
in the rubbled hollow of the home well
in the northern Somali Republic.

Off to the side – we swivel the camera –
where thorns are piled for the fence
the nomads are busy at their camp
fastening the huts with bark ropes.

One little hut that's new
arrived on the coarse grass from the sky.
It's the virgin spirit placed there somehow,
dazzling the nomads with the sunshine on it.

They sew up its door flaps with the ropes
so no man may crawl through
a tiny slit left at the bottom
like a button-hole in a Western shirt.

[*Dancing and film imagery influenced by Alice Walker's and Pratibha Parmar's work in West Africa.*]

58

Then on dry highlands of Somalia
we set their young girls to go dancing
in virginity round the sutured hut:
this is their sorrow in private places.

They dance in a hurt, stiff motion,
stick-legged as if avoiding stones
blood gleaming on brown thighs
tears in expressionless eyes.

The mouths of these children are silenced
by tradition: that they be made clean,
that they not become promiscuous,
that they be desirable for marriage

with a sewn vagina, stripped of pleasure,
crossed with thorns, as if the surgeons
had sutured the mouth of a healthy baby
leaving the palette uselessly cleft.

But this film is fantasy imagined from books
and my inability to suffer the thorns
that make religions stand erect, or that make
a temple's entrance so narrow.

We shoot the girls from a distance, telephoto,
forgetting the funds we raised in Britain,
forgetting the clan-lords warring in Mogadishu,
forgetting the entrenchment of Islam

into hard-line law, here called Shafi'i;
while the West threatens Islam with bombs
or rich products bearing our labels,
may our Jeeps not insult their culture.

We know these illiterates will never see our film;
so will the children make their children dance
that queer dance in this cinema-wilderness?
Our Jeep moves on, its tracks soon blown over.

The film is more penetrant than propaganda;
for it shows the silence here
and the thorny look in the girls' eyes;
it shows the male wind, harsh, hot.

Traditional Medicine: the Azande and Britain

There (is) a belief in this part of Africa (even among many whites, as I saw in Mozambique) that no man ever dies except by sorcery.

LACERDA, one-time Portuguese Astronomer Royal,
after an 18th century east coast voyage into the interior.

Evans-Pritchard says that for the Azande there is no such thing as an accidental death; all badness experienced by humans comes through witchcraft. Human life is caught in a web of beliefs:

a Zande cannot get out of its meshes because it is the only world he knows. The web is not an external structure in which he is enclosed. It is in the texture of his thought and he cannot think that his thought is wrong.

Our own medicine, for all its great advances, has lost an ancient spiritual richness hidden amid the worser aspects of this superstition. For the point extends far beyond witchcraft. Many traditional African societies were feudal, magical, and profoundly reflected a relationship between individual, communal and cosmic order. The kings did not possess their titles; rather, they inhabited their office. Somewhat as in European medieval times, each worker had his/her place, and the village with its shrines was laid out in a supernatural pattern which reflected this.

Deadly conservative, of course. But a Western prime minister or president's "sense of responsibility" is like a mere remnant of this, a tattered banner waved over an ethical wasteland. More Zairean music in my headphones...

The New Medicine

Three leading London hospitals have completed all the routine
treatments that the authorities had provided for that year

Hospitals too productive, come to the end of their budgets for ops,
routine surgery halted till the next budget, way of the world would mean
some bag lady didn't get her op, the bishop got his
with medical insurance like all higher-ups
on the internal market for organ repair.
Bank clerk not pushy, only a gristly testicular tumour, probably not him,
wasn't he nearly sixty, had to wait for a specialist, no big problem,
actress got her ovary op and a lot of attention in the media, bank clerk who?
He didn't die, you know, not him, these are not sentimental matters but bred in
the bone morals that what we do is sacred to each other, fat
chance. Baby mine, in memory, covered blue-black with staff infection,
nurses dabbing with calamine lotion, joking the sweetest jokes,
as the black invaded your neck.
What if those nurses had been infected by profit?
We have the money, you know, no problem. Baby, in memory still,
writhed on the bed, skin of a certain mottling, dried mackerel skin.
What if the baby ran into debt?
Should have looked where they were running when they voted for the bastards,
half a nation.
My mother voted for them, didn't look, had a mastectomy one time
but laughed when I said she had one breast in the grave now, and
medical insurance,
took an aneurism later, very cheery woman,
cheery being almost the highest moral gift because it beams outwards.
Price plays a part when the State chooses your hospital
no one gets the best without paying.
Nurse came to you, mother, like my conscience,
cool and neutral, warm and smiley, not like my restless individualism;
she built your body up in bed like a cornucopia riddled with it, conscience.
Have you had your medicine, man? said she to mother,
and I think of African lands where illness was a communal fault,
and witch doctors beat out psychiatrists in curing neuroses.
Oh but Britain's our medicine man, dying of its own accord.
Sometimes there's nothing to lift the heart from the death bed.
No grand causes left to fight for, said Osborne's old play.
But that's when the one cause becomes huge and obvious,

seen in the amused astral focus of the death principle:
our lives no more important than our deaths,
but by god you'd better get them both right on line,
no jumping the queue to live,
no pushing others forward in the queue to die.

Côte d'Ivoire

The old colonial official who lent me the African bow also used to let me borrow two pieces of ivory carved elaborately into eight-inch long sticks. Miniature magnifying glasses were set into the decorations to provide peep shows of equally-diminutive photographs in the recesses. In memory the sticks seem Indianesque, so perhaps Indians sold them in the local African ivory markets. Putting my eye to such a small aperture and seeing a foreign world would leave me today as childishly delighted as ever.

Big game hunting was not just a European "sport". Bantu tribes would trap and spear elephants for the Arabian trade long before the 19th century. In East Africa by medieval times, Arabian merchants traded African ivory, spices and Zandj slaves with China. In the Renaissance, the western bulge of Africa acquired names of colonialist greed: the Ivory Coast, the Gold Coast, and the Slave Coast.

By the 19th century European sporting hunters followed the missionaries as they opened up the African interior and stepped up animal slaughter by several factors. An ivory hunter called Edwards accompanied Robert Moffat on his visit to Mzilikazi of the Matabele in 1854. The cripple Jacob Hartley, hunting on horseback, claimed 1,200 elephants one year; William Finaughty once shot 95 elephants in a day; and two Boers returned from a safari with 10,000 lb of ivory.

All over Africa, the big game still retreat from us, even now when we are wanting at last to preserve them. A 1999 report from South Africa's Endangered Species Protection Unit shows that international treaties aimed at saving species in sub-Saharan Africa have made little impact. Now there's a scheme for making a limited ivory trade legal so that countries like Namibia, Botswana and Zimbabwe can sell stockpiles and use the proceeds for conserving elephants. Poaching and illegal traffic continue apace and funds have to come from somewhere to stop them; or, in another possibility, poaching will now increase.

Big Game

Carved baton of ivory,
a knick-knack, a mantelpiece gewgaw,
no longer than a skewer
has a glass lens inset, small as a jewel.

Peep in at a water-hole
and the eland get up, scattering;
peep in at forests of bamboo,
a baboon gone ancient with incomprehension;
peep in at a plain,
worn grass amid scrub tufts,
a lion cushioning its eyes as if with pain,
an elephant with trunk upraised
passing with its fellows, eye of huge humour,
feet placed down like the swinging imprimatur
of a rubber stamp,
the worn-out rubber of its hide
borne along after eons lying in sunny dust,
a covering thrown over a meat freight container
in a traffic jam of patient elephants,
tail quirt a loose end of pointy rope.
Then it's shot in the meaty shoulder,
keels over and shadowy figures
root out the tusks.

Peep in and see the red jungle drifting
with lianas raining blood down
across the centre of Africa, the pigmies
cowering under the rain of bullets,
the ribs of everything that's starving.

Nigeria: 1966, 1999

My adopted home, France, has headed off the US, my wife's nation, as world's leading exporter of conventional weapons while Britain ranks with Russia in the top four: I expect further jockeying for position as I write.

No one has the least idea what to do about this. Then we're looking at a "prize-winning" photograph of babies starving in the 1960s Biafran civil war, shown on French TV the other night.

Like many another African country, Nigeria's troubles began when the national boundaries were drawn in colonial times. At independence, the Nigerian federation brought three main groups into uneasy cohabitation: the Islamic Hausa-Fulani in the north; the Yoruba tribal system in the west and south-west; and the talented, decentralised Ibo in the south-east, where the breakaway Biafra was concentrated. But depending on counting procedures, Nigeria has from 200 to 400 ethnic groups, of which ten comprise 90 per cent of the population; the Middle Belt is especially complicated. The crucial oilfields are in the south.

In 1966-67, after an Ibo-led coup, a Muslim-sparked counter-coup pitchforked to power Lt-Col. Gowon, a Middle Belt Christian. As this failed to end persecution of Ibos by the north; the Ibos broke away from the federation and proclaimed their brief-lived state of Biafra.

Only half of Britain accepted the Wilson government's view that the war should be shortened by supplying arms to federal Nigeria, who were clearly going to win. The French supported Biafra and Israel gave material support. Egyptian pilots flew for the federal airforce. South Africa and white Rhodesia supported Biafra; the Organisation of African Unity sought an integrated Nigeria. The Chinese aided Biafra to counteract Soviet support for the federal side.

I believe Harold Wilson's memoirs where he talks of acute moral dilemma as the British Press stormed against his pro-Federal policies. The dilemma was slicked by British interests in the southern oilfields for which Nigeria and Biafra were battling. I remain baffled by these questions.

In modern times, a northern military dictatorship seized power after a previous military regime annulled a democratic presidential election. An international scandal centring on the oil-rich Ogoni region to the south led to Nigeria's suspension from the Commonwealth. The Ogonis claimed that the Shell petrochemicals conglomerate extracted $30 billion worth of oil from their region over 40 years and in return have left behind pollution and neglect.

The government bore down heavily on Ogoni protest: hundreds died, the military occupied the region, and the hanging of nine protesters against the ecological disaster, including the writer Ken Saro-Wiwa, led to Commonwealth reprisals against Nigeria.

The Shell company, which kept a low profile, was fiercely criticised for self-interested inaction and, in that sense, supporting the regime. In my introduction I cited *Newsweek*'s suggestion that under trade deregulation multinationals might become the most powerful social glue left in a world without ideology. The example of Nigeria is a measure of such hopes. Transnational business ethics dictate non-interference in a country's internal politics if that interrupts trade. Unfortunately, whether Shell like it or not, their oil operations have enormously influenced Nigerian politics and ecology: no business that size can be value-neutral.

As for arms, nearly two years after that modern coup, Britain was publicly reviling the military dictatorship while still fulfilling an existing contract to sell it tanks. Couldn't offend against the terms of a business contract. 'Ethics.' In Western exploitation of Nigerian oil and in our arms sales we – like Nigeria's northern peoples – are now as heavily indebted to the Ogoni as we were earlier to the Ibos of Biafra.

The Nobelist poet-playwright, Wole Soyinka, conscience of his nation, said in an interview:

> Although I insist on placing the maximum blame for the Nigerian crisis on our own lack of leadership and vision, it is the evil seeds which Britain planted in our continent that have now blossomed into these poisoned fruits. Britain needs to apologise on many levels.

Or the voice of Saro-Wiwa comes to us, reported by Rob Nixon:

> Saro-Wiwa has likened the fate of the Ogoni during the oil-rush to their fate in the Biafran War, when the conflict among Nigeria's three dominant ethnicities left them flattened 'like grass in the fight of the elephants'. In a military kleptocracy with two hundred minority groups, all constitutionally unprotected, the Ogonis suffered the extra misfortune of living over oil.

With the recent death of the dictator, General Abacha, the military has at last permitted elections and General Olusegun Obasanjo has thereupon joined the club of former African military rulers now returned to civilian power. In consequence, Nigeria has come out of the international cold, and, with the World Bank newly involved, its once $29 billion external debt will no doubt be rescheduled. The future of this nation, so vital to the health of West Africa, remains uneasy. Soyinka has just returned to his country, a good sign.

The Lurch into Neutrality

I've dined with British diplomats.
uncommonly handsome, tall, Edenish,
with the same retiring quick-wittedness and decency
the flashy anger of ambition never shown.
They're cleverer than me, more suave,
readier with compliments:
'So-and-so was awfully good in Beirut.
Nigel's back from Kuala Lumpur.'
In such professionalism, their predecessors
invented African countries,
scoring straight lines between tribal systems
they could pass exams in,
bargaining with chiefs, establishing a nation
not their own, say Nigeria,
across ancient kingdoms.

Then Nigeria at civil war
touched my life briefly
in the University Arms, Cambridge.
A novice reporter
for the *Cambridge Evening News*,
I was cornered in the hotel lounge
by three propagandists from Ibo-run Biafra,
a country shining new with righteousness,
cutting across colonial partitions.
Chinua Achebe could have been one of the three;
anyway, his stories catch that moment of promise,
and the war stopped his friend, Okigbo,
in the middle of his thunderous poetic drum-roll.
Outside the hotel, cricketers cracked
a ball or two on Parker's Piece,
but I was all these diplomats had,
so they bowled at me gracefully.
They told me of famines and atrocities,
of British iniquity in supplying
arms to Nigeria's Gowon,
in fostering military action
against this small Biafra,
struggling against corruption.

For premier Harold Wilson in his memoirs,
this was outstanding Biafran PR.
Britain was 'traditional arms supplier'
to Nigeria (eight years old).
Stopping would mean support for Biafra,
not a 'lurch into neutrality'.
Ten percent of British oil
coming then from Nigeria,
this war making sterling shaky.

Biafra's fate was strung
in a cat's cradle of British interests,
the strings we'd twined so long ago
subtended from outside Nigeria's borders.

I read the memoirs with a sinking heart
the other day, whereas that summer,
I rose from my hotel armchair bewildered.
I knew so little of Biafra:
how could I report its diplomats, one-sided?
How could I deny their case either?
My story made four inches,
the very measure of my caution.

A quarter-century later,
Nigeria grew greasy with its oil,
military or tribal corruption, nepotism,
British papers lapped up its scandals.
Nigerian artists were placed in danger,
Saro-Wiwa hanged, Soyinka forced abroad.
This morning I re-read Achebe's
A Man of the People,
where Biafra's troubles lie in germ.
Don't you, the reader, wish that I, the poet,
could walk back into that hotel lounge,
sit down and listen to those men?
And I say
there are cradles of string, strings of words,
we never can undo,
and this present string of words is one of them.

Rwanda: Doom-saying Africa

Now we have broached the cask of tragedies we might as well sup full of them, for they have afflicted most of the old colonial territories, French, Portuguese, and Belgian as well as British, and also Liberia and Sierra Leone, each known in the 19th century as territories for freed slaves.

An article by the US writer, Robert Kaplan, in *The Atlantic Monthly* was so full of doom for Africa that it became quickly notorious. He compares West African prospects to those in Europe during the Thirty Years' War, with the post-colonial governments in constant collapse, warlords battling it out over terrains of disease, populations increasing out of control or wandering homeless across desolate landscapes. Mercenaries have been employed as "peacekeepers". Westerners love this stuff.

Commenting in the *Trib*, William Pfaff talks of post-colonial Africa, along with Russia and the Balkans, as situations where 'overarmed and culturally uprooted men create a moral moonscape.' Interpol says organised crime has turned to West African countries – there's a new Interpol office in Abidjan (Côte d'Ivoire) – and one big danger is a drug network linking West Africa, its suppliers in South America and Asia, and consumer markets in Europe and the United States.

The notorious Hutu massacre campaign in Rwanda was not one whit mitigated, of course, by centuries of French interference in Rwanda and Burundi or by the destabilising effects of international financial restructuring shortly before the genocide. The consequences are still playing out in the Congo.

Much that happens in Africa is *sui generis*, but much happens too as a distant effect of world capitalism. Industrial nations are hard at work creating their own planetary "moral moonscape": global free trade threatens to destroy social structures in favour of a vague, anarchistic internationalism

Jeremy Harding writing in *The London Review of Books* cites Rosa Luxemburg's warning that capitalism might lead to barbarism. And of course he adds that capitalism is not the only enemy of the African nation-states: their governments themselves so often will not govern responsibly or justly or humanely. The whole question of African recovery rests on the tremulous balance between good government and good aid.

The Tapestry

A great relic up for sale, Europe's still
an ornate palace, courtyards ruled by stars,
ringed by balconies with stone torsos,
doors black wood with Renaissance trim of gold.
Businessmen's consortia, anxiety's consumers,
have emptied this palace thing of spiritual life; so
another thing, deathy, skulks in secret passages.
"Committee" doors block entrances guarded by
cartoon toecaps with crescent bootblack highlights.

Past these doors the palace tapestries are tattered,
one's a *mille feuille* parody. Birds on the boughs
shoulder each other like a tight line of soldiers
and peck at sticky pinks, wasps among nectared blues,
a red-gowned woman fattens into opulence.
The next's a horror; it shows chemical smoke
in another land, Guinea or Rwanda.
Birds pipe piteously on contorted branches,
scars of white on cindered trunks.

The deathy thing has come among us,
heritor of palace policy. The tapestry lifts
and there the thing is: a rubber wall panel
with a hole leading to death's passageways.
Climbing through, we step down stairs
walled with dusty scars. A musty smell:
we find a boot charred by war, a fragment
of webbing; through a door we see explosions
in wiry tree tops, a missile corkscrewing off.

Out there, fleeing chiefs leave farms vacant,
oxen no longer plough for the seasonal crop.
By stripped roots lie two long canteen tins
each containing a mummified child
in cobwebs, leathern flesh stretched from
eye sockets, bony fetish dolls whose hearts
bristle with nails. We've made enemies
of hairless homunculi little in their thunders,
bugballs created by African wars.

Cape Verde Islands: the 1980s

A dangerous saying of the German philosopher, Scheler, has obsessed me for a lifetime:

> The man who thinks historically and systematically approaches ideal and exact images better than a man impelled by tradition.

Nation-building can never be performed well historically and systematically. Sometimes, it is the most brilliant leaders whom these exact images seduce.

Africa's post-independence failures make a grievous list: Ghana with its noble, foundering vision; Tanzania or Mozambique with their Africanised socialism; Ethiopia with its cruder, brutal Marxism; Lumumba's post-independence Congo/Zaire caught instantly between American and Russian ambitions and Belgian intrigue; Sekou Touré's Guinea which battled alone and unsuccessfully to do without Gaullist French paternalism.

The list grows longer, Cuban or South African backed conflict in Angola still continuing with other backers, Siad Barre's "scientific socialism" in Somalia breaking up into the 1990s' clan war...

Could there be a country small enough for thorough socialism to work?

Try the Cape Verde Islands off Africa's north-west shoulder, where Sir John Hawkins lay at anchor so long ago. In classical myth, these were the isles beyond the western wind, where the nymphs of Hesperus fed on golden apples in bowers guarded by a dragon. A less mythical dragon arrived in the shape of the Portuguese, who used the islands as human storage before they shipped their slaves.

Because of Portugal's Fascism, Guinea-Bissau and Cape Verde only won independence in 1974, when the PAIGC revolutionary party took control of both former colonies. Cape Verde socialism was inspired by that purest of revolutionaries, Amilcar Cabral of Guinea-Bissau, assassinated by Salazar's regime just before independence.

With a coup in 1980, the pure revolution in Guinea-Bissau fell prey to the tensions of West Africa (tensions that have engulfed Liberia and Sierra Leone in two of the worst civil wars). In the Cape Verde islands, just across the water, the party split from Guinea-Bissau and changed the initials of its name slightly. An intense, short-lived democracy was installed, a story I tell almost in prose.

Sailing to the Fortunate Isles

We set sail on a voyage of socialism,
a freer page or two in the vast log
of slavery by capture, by armies, religions,
colonialism, or western bankers.
We're idling on the water, thinking of
veteran followers of Amilcar Cabral
as they carry the struggle peacefully
to the golden islands of Cape Verde.

For one, bright revolutionary moment,
the sails spring taut in people's minds,
hope blows through, generosity,
groups forming everywhere;
the Portuguese retire. We fear
what happens next: the wind dies down;
the people tire of a dawdling economy
guided by inexpert popular meetings and high
advice from party officials while droughts
destroy the maize and bean crops.
The Catholics take over, their best
turn of the heart is charity.

But suppose my hand, creating these journeys,
hasn't yet stirred, suppose the sails
are still slack. Then visions precede events:
dreams rise like islands we imagine:
volcanic rock sheer from the Atlantic,
distant from West Africa's greenest cape.
As soon as caravels creak in trade winds
the cargo will be slaves: Portuguese
hatches battened down on nauseous stench,
pit-minted leg irons, the slaves
jostled in the hot fate of being shipped off,
the masters' counting every man-jack,
seal coughs of escapees in mountain clefts,
bullet streaks on rockfaces.

Suppose none of this happening
yet, or perhaps it happened once
in other islands. Suppose
a breeze truly originary.

Offshore from green capes pleated by tree trunks,
sailing beyond the setting sun's arms
spread on the Western skyline,
we discover ourselves
on these islands called "Fortunate".
We stop in a street our dream makes,
pick up a windfall by a fence, a golden apple,
and bite on it, looking round for inhabitants
the apple chunks curious in our mouths.

While there's no air for humans
in the subdued light with the sun
gone down on the washed horizon,
something of the gold persists
as a plating on window glass in the fuzzy
buildings of these over-perfect islands,
more perfect than in Cabral's
humane polity of little public meetings.

Our fullest hope is the emptiest potential,
and we take our apple naturally
up its streets. Islanders disappear
round corners hazing the streets
with their presence. We pause
at political murmurs in a classroom.
Are those the peasants seeking
reforms from reluctant landlords?
The desks gleam with lost
sunlight; on the blackboard rectangles
chalked beside the initials PAIVC;
but the chalk fades rapidly after
a lesson just given. The Catholic
bell dins. We let the apple fall.

What has never happened yet,
the ideal, will not survive
its arrival, already it has always
lasted like a bitten apple rolling
down an endless golden road.

Mozambique: Socialism's Unlevel Playing Field

Socialism had a far worse history in Mozambique. There, Samora Machel's Frelimo party set up a constitution uniting party and nation, with a polit-bureau and party branches reaching down to provincial, district and sub-districts, carrying the message into factories, institutions, schools, defence forces and neighbourhoods. Like Tanzania, Mozambique displaced peasants into communal villages: the disaffected broke away to form their own hamlets.

Photographs prompt misleading nostalgia: outside the 'Dynamising Group' offices a party worker harangues a mass meeting, the forest of raised arms, the peasant woman's face rapt after voting, the people dancing in communal joy.

As usual under too optimistic a socialism, nothing worked properly and the West became hostile. All went haywire dreadfully into civil war, economic collapse, and starvation; Machel was assassinated.

All along, Mozambique had played a contradictory role: acting as the copper export route across southern Africa via Maputo (Lourenço Marques), it was also a front-line state battling South African apartheid. White supremacy retaliation was all too simple. The carrier trade with white-minority-run Rhodesia closed down; South Africa sent only low tariff goods and diverted high tariff shipments elsewhere; Maputo's transit business collapsed. Rhodesia and South Africa, with covert CIA support, fomented right-wing banditry within Mozambique and South Africa massed troops on the border, so that scarce resources were swallowed up by meeting the invasion threat.

Southern Africa's front-line states paid heavily for fighting apartheid when they themselves were wrestling with disasters, partly caused by Western opposition to their socialism, partly caused by their own dangerous purity.

Mozambique

The soldiers' heelmarks filled with dust, the war
crept on, the shadow of the Portuguese retreating left
the sunny land too dry, revealed the bare treasury,
the bankrupt independence. There's sand still shelving
in Samora Machel's footfall, such a mark he left

on Mozambique, a rigid purity, his heels
resounding on a rostrum, single fist held high
as if in ardour for his heart-winning tongue,
and in ardour for committees, trying to link a people,
largely illiterate, to all that Frelimo fought for.

The Party a tent-pole in a land of huts,
no canvas covering it under Frelimo's sun,
some shirted lecturer among sticks, his fingers
counting out directives, the audience so poor
frayed singlets ran in rivers on their backs.

The Portuguese had trained no one to run farms,
left no investment capital, South Africa
withdrew its gold, a crisis from the very start,
western hands withdrawing within gold-linked
shirt-cuffs, or proffering ruinous loans.

Immediately, free-traders and the apartheid-mouthed,
the CIA, South Africa, Smith's Rhodesia, the sorry gang,
began their sabotage, they funded rebel rightists and
the Catholic Church, a pro-colonialist enemy, knew
their God hates Marxists; God sent a drought on cue.

New war inside the arid land; outside its borders
lay racism's front-line; a million people were to die.
Party officials went desperate from its Congress,
to hillsides, to breakaway villages; they brought
not goods but party directives, even the sjambok.

Soon the free market powers had fomented anarchy
in a situation already doomed to it. Stood back:
'You see what Marxism has done!' Mozambique prey
to World Bank receivers – very inconvenient
for trade when Maputo's great port stood idle.

The Northern sky went black with money signatures
sent via computer passwords, becoming shadow entities
flocking like starlings up to satellites from Washington
to the far side of the world; whitening, the bills
flew down to roost in favoured trees, Tokyo, Riyadh, Bonn –

flew far north from these treeless badlands technologised
at night; red cliffs by day going grey under a moon
like a CD rim above a forgotten, leopard-freckled nation;
bony okapis stumbled on the hills, vultures
limped, trailing their scraggy cloaks of greed.

On the Northern side of the world, shadowy men
marshalled us Britons into their army of wealth;
our civil bullets fired south into starving lands
and spoke to those fallen on sand: 'You've lost me, Sir,
in your eyes, where I have found your h-he-heart.'

They died by Machel's heelmark. Frelimo now distrusted
his purity. Ah, then the West came from the shadows
with fistfuls of loans, fomenting elections where
apostasy-Marxists faced murderous rightists,
with a billion bankers' dollars to stabilise democracy.

In blazer green fields now is another Mozambique,
a woman twin-gunned with crimson watering cans;
beside her, footmarks, a crooked hand planting seeds
into a line of words growing against the hunger.
Plant this, water this, a crop truly green.

Ghana: the Ironies of Success

Nkrumah's pan-Africanism was the grandest vision. From his student days on, Nkrumah developed Garveyite ideas into a continent-wide sense of racial unity, inspiring radicals everywhere including young resistance fighters in South Africa. And in 1957 he led Ghana to become the first sub-Saharan nation to gain independence from modern colonialism. Our debt to him for that remains, whatever happened later.

Once he was in power, his fully socialist nation gradually declined into authoritarianism, a failed economy, and a plethora of state organisations. He claimed that Britain and the US forced down Ghana's cocoa prices after 1961 to destabilise his costly reforms. A conspiracy is highly unlikely. Without encouragement, Western markets go hostile in the face of African socialism.

Today, under the presidency of Jerry Rawlings, Ghana is the flagship for IMF and World Bank's claims that free market budgeting will rescue African economies. After a cruel beginning, the energetic regime has stabilised the nation and investment and loans are newly available.

At times, world gold prices have allowed Ghana to step up mining. Gold, the country's ancient source of wealth, is also the international capitalist crop *par excellence*. And the cost, therefore, has been a slightly increased loss of sovereignty. The government fairly recently finished off selling 55 percent of the famous Ashanti (Asante) Goldfields, raising about $400 million to aid recovery. Britain's Lonrho has become major shareholder of a company with a market capitalisation of about $1.8 billion, according to *The Wall Street Journal*. This is the irony of gaining in power by losing it to foreigners.

Monetarist policies rarely share out wealth fairly or, at least, quickly: while a new infrastructure is under construction, the poor, especially in rural areas, will have to wait to see much profit.

I saw Rawlings being greeted by a hostile Ghanaian street demonstration as he visited London's Centre Point building in Tottenham Court Road. They had not forgiven him for the executions conducted when he seized power. A Ghanaian businessman stood to one side scornfully. When I asked him what he thought, he sneered that the demonstrators did not realise Rawlings's achievements. Now, at last, he himself could go home, he said. It took tens of years – a hundred perhaps – to build a new country solidly, and those who didn't understand this were childish.

There are two sides to these ironies.

Ghana of Gold and Cocoa

Nkrumah one moment lent Africa his face;
it had the eidetic sheen that glistens with
the immediate and uncertain, leaving in mind
his bush of hair like the western bulge
of a continent made one in its Africanness.

Skilled at being great, he saw Ghana
as a state corporate jig-saw piece of an Africa
joggling its ill-fitting puzzle into unity.
His grandeur diminished, with lost authority,
failure in cocoa prices, and with leaders' graft.

The soil cracked in fierce sunlight, the harmattan
lit the bush with casual fires, and ploughs
on plantations stood up on their heels,
the oxen idled, great wheels were motionless
in the gold mines run by hopeless corporations.

Footprints in history's richer dust were leading
towards Ghana's hinterland, empty lanes winding
among mud huts, interior walls painted
in zigzags, brush-stroke ladders, kente cloth
hung and billowing, jiggering staggered patterns.

For much was ideology, West Africa on a book
seen as his wonderful face looking sideways,
calling for freedom as we always must; but
we know that soldiers come later if the soil's
brown stew boils dry leaving khaki fibres.

And Nkrumah's great spell boiled away
in a seven-year drought, as the economy plummeted,
and coup, then, could only be answered with coup,
until weapons gleamed with fresh oil; grenades
crocodilian in their skin were unglued from the teeth

to be thrown by younger soldiers, new radicals
who captured the radio heart of Accra: bullets
thudded into the bodies of the old guard. When Ghana
settled its accounts the world's face turned away
from this vicious codicil to Nkrumah's testament.

After the last shots fired down the river, a calm
in the writhings of the current, gnats whined
within the inlets where cocoa sheen lay
on stagnant surfaces; in the capital,
big men in borrowed robes went to be executed.

Ghana of gold and cocoa, the colours now
are freshly painted in the huts; the gold light slides
up windows of office blocks awakening in Accra;
the Volta shrugs itself free of terror and the current
muscles onwards bearing the lights along;

the ploughs dig in the plantations; the wheels
are turning again; the children run
past the painted zigzags; downriver
foreign capitalists peer into mirrors of gold
to see their own face. Gold rarely carries upriver.

Togo: Hardly Socialistic

I like to maintain a loose, non-dogmatic definition of socialism: broadly, no one fully owns the wealth they take out of a society; at most, it is permitted to them. The definition would tolerate any governmental system that can create fairness without cruelty.

Similarly, Triad nations do not fully own the wealth they draw out of the poorer parts of the world.

A workable system for redistributing wealth hasn't been discovered; neither dogmatic socialism nor global free trading in their purities are likely to achieve this goal. But those who squawk of the death of socialism are mechanical toy parrots. It's like saying romanticism in poetry has been defeated by classicism. If socialism were "romantic", free market economics would be "classical"; and Adam Smithite liberal economics are indeed called "classical". Like literary neo-classicism of the 18th century, they depend upon the idea that a natural law or order (invisible hand of God) underlies the apparently chance results of vigorous, "natural" competition.

Hard-bitten free traders often don't acknowledge this almost-religious under-surface of their realism, though something has to explain the light in their eyes.

As in poetry, economic "classicism" can never finally defeat "romanticism", or vice-versa. If either tendency – socialistic or free market – could keep economic vitality, fight pollution, and distribute wealth fairly we would probably have solved most other political arguments by fairy wand. (The status of women and racial questions are other matters for which we need the socialist view.)

Models of African development run promptly into political naivety. One form refuses to acknowledge the world failure of socialist systems. Another would sentimentalise African village life, with all its noble communal sense, timelessness of the life-cycle, and would ignore the things it so often lacks: possessions, political freedom, aspiration, hope of advancement, food and medicine.

Equally grave is the disguised naivety of international experts, the worldly-wise who presume that by allowing African nations open access to our markets those village societies are willingly going to become just like us, with the same aspirations. Then, like the old missionaries, we will have saved them.

Another naivety is, frankly, my own: my wish that our Northern power groups do not enforce our own economic and technological image upon a continent. Naive because I don't know how to stop the process. I only know it is arrogant and greedy.

Few Possessions in Togo

If we think about rural lands, it's night
more swiftly over village earth humid
with vegetal rotting. Our feet halt. After
the manioc-pounded day, the hot yam
fields haunched with women, the blaze
has gone out of it, a hand-wave of light
behind the black rectangles, unglassed,
cut into mud or concrete huts, creates

a dream of few possessions, the kerosene
lamp by an enamel cooking pot, the fufu
in it bland as tofu. It's our eye at
the glimmering window, where, halted,
we pick up the gleam of French fashion
mag pics on the interior wall, above
a single stool, kids already foetal
for sleep, knees up to swollen bellies.

The hard floor bare, a wooden toy,
the man out somewhere topping up
with palm wine, and the mother
easing her spine after the day's bending.
What can we add to so little, us with
what we think is so much?
We leave a nothing by the mud wall; it's
the oval trademark in a Western shoeprint.

The Bemba of Zambia: 19th Century to Modern Times

> The optical-fibre networks that are currently being laid across the
> United States and, more slowly, elsewhere, are capable of carrying
> hundreds of thousands of times more traffic than the traditional
> copper wire.
>
> WILLIAM SHAWCROSS, *Murdoch*

Though new technologies destabilise distant economies so casually, what
could replace the beauty of copper, most characteristic of African metals?

The Bemba

Night in Northern history, a single railway
stretched north across the copper belt,

hundreds of campfires lined out in darkness
as Africans waited for the dawn of white industry,

the conductivity of copper, the wires of it
spiralling outwards and shivering across the world.

The beauty of the view in copper surfaces,
red gilded as it burnishes the fact,

reflected people moving like a leaking
of colour in a scene they're always part of,

a saucepan copper alloy perhaps
originating south of Katanga

in mines of Kitwe, Chingola, Mufulira,
where the modern Bemba work.

Once a people of stockaded villages
on an arid plain, the Bemba went on border raids,

started small wars, bound stolen
filaments round wrists and ankles.

In a second-hand notion of their history,
nostalgic distortion,

as if the keenness of spear wounds or 19th century
shouts of sharp triumph on the grasslands

could still be seen moving, mute, painless,
in reflections slinking round the saucepans

unthreatened by Zambia's modern economic wars
against Chile's, Russia's, America's

copper on world markets. No Bemba, no borders,
are mentioned in money signs flickering along the wires.

Uganda and the Hyena

Amin's ghost is slowly fading from Uganda. Maureen Johnson reporting for Associated Press says that the former dictator, now in his 70s, is living in luxury with several wives, masses of children, servants and cars in the Red Sea port of Jeddah, Saudi Arabia, where he can spotted walking along the coast or attending Friday prayers in the mosque. The Saudis pick up his hefty bills in exchange for his silence.

In the 1970s I reviewed for *The African Book Publishing Record* a biting animal-story by Alumidi Osinya called *Field Marshal Abdulla Salim Fisi (Or How the Hyena Got His!)*. It takes wing from African animal fables and satirises Ugandan leaders since the time of the old Kabaka of Buganda (the lion) down through that of Obote (the leopard) to the rule of Amin (the hyena).

About that time, in Amin's palace a BBC TV interviewer asked the dictator about human rights reports of thousands of people gone 'missing'. Amin joked back to the effect that there was no evidence in his palace of any missing people; 'You don't see any here,' or something like that. Toady aides guffawed in the background. In Osinya's novel, *Field Marshal Abdullah Salim Fisi*, asked about bloodbaths, responds: 'Did you find any bath in my house full of blood?'

Though Uganda only a year or two back seemed full of new promise, its tribal problems have not ended. Since I wrote this poem, rebellion from northern and western tribes has forced President Yoweri Museveni to tighten his grip on his one-party state, and he has involved his country in the present Congo war. But, then again, the energy and excellence of his campaigns to prevent HIV infection provide one motive to trust his governance.

On Learning a Wary Trust

The military saviour's spine is over-straight,
like a full-bellied sideboard, comportment
of a chief. Museveni of Uganda on TV
smiles warily, speaks of grounds for hope,
after Obote, Amin, the slaughtering.
'Not even Rwanda has the numbers
massacred which we... absorbed,'
says Museveni evenly into camera
but he's overtaken by the Rwandan news.
Joyful but equally warily, Ugandans,
decimated by past cruelties,
and by AIDS, swallow single-party politics
again and remember how to trust.
Even the World Bank coughs up.

Moonlight fogged the window frost.
In my nightmare Amin's concrete
prisons suddenly dashed with blood.
Crossing the bedroom, barefoot,
I was the author of my silhouette
against the whitened glass,
a shadow of anyone real,
straight-spined, full-bellied as I am,
if seen from the street outside
in an empty English fishing village.

When I rubbed a spyhole in the frost
the overcoated man was there already –
he's the one who comes at night
into the streets of our self-absorbed romance
for us to have a transaction of glances
between our inner hollow and the man's
malevolence. I'm telling you,
that man was real; also, he appeared
in the nightmare's closing fiction.
Immediately normal courage
filled the moral hollow, he moved
away from the window-view,
as Amin moved away from Uganda
when the people's courage rose.

Swaziland

After flickering across the central and northern faces of Africa it is time to turn south.

I've been puzzling over the history of three small independent countries which, with British backing, managed to resist being swallowed up by white South Africa: Swaziland, Lesotho and Botswana.

Nowadays, we're well aware of the health risk from asbestos, a material familiar for much of my life. Until I began reading about Swaziland, a little spot on the map where South Africa meets Mozambique, I'd never known where our asbestos came from, or who had unknowingly taken the risks of mining it – who had placed me in that debt.

When I read my poem 'The Infibulation Ceremony' in the Royal Albert Hall a couple of years back, an African commissionaire chuckled pleasantly as I left: 'You'll be writing a poem about Swaziland next!' I didn't have the nerve to tell him I had already written one.

Protection from the Heat

Near the Lansdowne, Bournemouth,
new paypacket, farm machinery reporter,
£70 a month, dressing in Willoughby suits,
new shirts, a snap-brim hat, a real twit
back South from the Royal Highland Show
and talking about sugar-beet harvesters.
My father's iron repasses, brings silk to life
on the browned cloth of the board,
upends on a steel-cratered asbestos pad
worn down by many irons. It's a
memory in a kitchen, a bald-headed
man named after the Gordon Highlanders
ironing large silk underpants, 1963,
while he listens grimly to prattle.

Irons often repass but the full life
within us is never smoothed.
Underground in Swaziland, miners
were hacking at chrysotile asbestos,
breathing-in the needled dust,
for five pounds fifteen shillings
and tenpence a month, plus benefits,
from owners, Turner & Newall,
the British fighting unions in Africa
which they couldn't fight at home.
Injustice makes us gasp first,
then enters the lungs like tiredness.

Offered a seventh of my wage that year
the miners struck; and Swazi politics
took wing. Out came sugar ranch workers,
then domestics, labourers marching in streets,
Lord Lansdowne, Colonial Minister of State,
protected from marchers by tear gas,
stalled a constitution for British reasons,
the Swazi king temporising in the middle.

They brought in the Gordon Highlanders
from Kenya. What the hell did the Scots
soldiers think they were doing there,
strike-breaking, rounding up tax offenders,
or those who fled South African torturers?
Swazi independence politicians went to jail
for carefully judged sentences.
Wages hiccuped upwards, just a bit,
a modern state was born, the king
held on to power, foreigners went on
grabbing riches in the Swazi mountains,
huge stocks of pig iron, coal,
shunted out by rail through Mozambique.

I know the poem has a weak foundation:
Asbestos as its theme, or difference in wages,
some mere coincidence in words: sugar,
Lansdowne, Scotland, Gordon, the iron
repassing, nothing rendered smooth
except easy silk, the difficult renewal
of a nation never a full renewal,
asbestos now recognised a danger.
I expect they're still going, Turner & Newall,
and I am still going, still somewhat a fool.

Lesotho: A Praise Song

A verbatim autobiography recorded by John and Cassandra Perry from Stimela Jason Jingoes, a Lesotho resident who lived a very varied life, contains this praise song:

> Litongwa of Mavuso, fall down
> That the people may drink water.
> You, Mtshengu of Tshabalala,
> You, Mtshengu, talked
> To the men at the court and they trembled.
> You, the sons of Sikova, the Owl,
> Who has horns like a heifer,
> You great liars:
> You reported that the Chief was dead
> When he was not dead.
> You of dirty dresses,
> Who can be buried at your mother's place;
> You who pledge on the cobra snake
> and say it is your clan;
> you of loud applause,
> What can you do to Mswati, the Swazi,
> Who is a bull?

'These are the praises of my ancestors, who are Swazi,' says Jingoes. 'When I meet another Swazi, especially one of my clan, the clan of the cobra, we sing these praises together, and we cry. This is the history of my forefathers as it has been told to me.'

It turns out to be a *roman à clé*. For instance, in the ancestral past, Gatagata, denied the clan Chieftainship by Sitinga, moved with his followers away from the maternal home – hence the line about 'your mother's place'. Or again, on one occasion, the breakaway group announced the death of Gatagata's younger brother to Sitinga, but out of respect for the dead, said only 'the Prince' had died, mentioning no name. Sitinga's people thought that 'the Prince' meant Gatagata, but then they discovered that Gatagata was still alive and called the breakaway group 'great liars" who had been secretly preparing an invasion by pretending that their leader was dead.

Ancestor Worship

A grandmother wanders the foothills
in a dream of Lesotho, nation of starry mountains.
She approaches downhill, wearing a mohair blanket
with a cradle-skin under it, beads on her head
as in the old days. Her face is light-skinned,
Swazi-featured and cratered with anguish,
like the land eroding down by the rivers.
She asks a Mosotho, a grandson, dreaming,
for a black cow with white face and tail
to appease her hunger when it's sacrificed.
Having to seek work in the Boer world,
he lies sleeping in the Western Transvaal
where such a beast, parti-coloured, can be found
on a white man's farm; but the farmer won't sell,
for his wife loves the cow, emblem of fortune.

Why do these ancestors ask us in dreams
for pledges we can't truthfully fulfil?
They won't let us worship their old lives,
keeping it fond in memory, but worry us
with the patched consistency of our new lives.
In a waking dream my Scottish grandmother,
approaching from the stern patriarchy of church
down the foothills of the Clyde, asks me
the unforgivable, to be true to conservative
cultures that won't sell the cow. She taught
me to read, but all I've read betrays her
and, she implies in the dream, is hellish.
Her spirit drifts onto me like a wreath of mist
that tires my legs suddenly, for I can't escape
this dragging of a revered inheritance.

Couldn't a sacrifice be made in two nations,
redeeming the pledge in Lesotho
in worship of my own grandmother?
As if I should buy a cow with black body
and send only its white head to the abattoir,
and do this for the rigid Scottish matriarch?

Such truthfulness would send her horrified
from my dreams and the Lesotho spirits
would writhe around me in their mists.
I'm so tired, not great-souled enough
to worship ancestors, though it must be done,
some way be found. Therefore I sacrifice
for the two grandmothers dressed in cradle-skin
this poem, parti-coloured in its reverence,
black in its body, white in face and tail.

Botswana: A Diamond on the Finger

As with the very different regime in Ghana, there's a good capitalist explanation for the success of little Botswana: not gold this time, but diamonds. When diamond prices rise world-wide, this product can account for three-quarters of total export income in good years, attracting considerable South African and US investment. The government has negotiated agreements giving them 70 percent of mining profits. If you've got the metals and minerals and allow the foreigners in, any government can be a success.

A more human story lies behind the creation of independent Botswana, a story of the kind newspapers love to tell.

There was a "Great" Khama, Khama I, who founded the nation by uniting the Tswana and Khoi-San groups in the 1870s and who persuaded Joseph Chamberlain in Britain to make the country a protectorate in 1891. This would save "Bechuanaland" from Rhodes's men and Afrikaners only too anxious for land and gold.

Khama's grandson, Seretse, caused an international scandal when, as a law student in London, he became engaged to Ruth Williams, a British nurse and married her in a Chelsea registry office.

Seretse Khama's regent, his formidable uncle, Tshekedi Khama, was outraged. Worried about his nation and fearful that Britain might prevent Seretse from becoming chief, Tshekedi resigned the regency in protest against this marriage's violation of tribal custom. The South Africans, for their part, couldn't stand a mixed marriage right there on their borders and pressured Britain economically and politically to take action. Against everything the Labour Party was supposed to stand for, Attlee's government behaved like snakes in the grass.

Seretse was invited back to London in 1950 to talk with the Secretary of State for Commonwealth Relations about 'the future administration of the Bamangwato' (his tribe). As a precaution, Ruth remained in Serowe. The Secretary offered Seretse £1,000 a year tax free if he would live in England, renounce his chieftainship, and thus keep the plague of miscegenation from South Africa's borders. Seretse refused to give in; the British exiled him from the Protectorate and stripped him of his chieftainship.

The British eventually allowed both Khamas to return as private citizens and to participate in tribal affairs. In 1958, the two of them initiated the move which led to independence as a republic and in 1965 elections Seretse Khama, now heading a political party, was a shoe-in for Prime Minister. Ever-ready Britain knighted him and he became a rigidly conservative, but undeniably successful, president in 1966.

Rapid growth in mining and cattle industries has led to the unequal distribution of wealth that one would expect in a society divided by class; and the Khoi-San life style is having a hard time surviving. Yet, diamonds apart, much of modern Botswana's original stability had its basis in Seretse's resolute personality and incarnation of the ancient tribal hierarchies.

The Mixed Marriage

We've made an inhuman narrative of the world,
a story figured into computer games;
I pass through hollow arcades where
heroes and heroines are financiers
practising their martial arts
in bodies formed of triangular pixels
like miniature trade cartels. They speak
as diplomats do with synthesised voices,
language feeds off randomised language,
pee-tchow, pee-tchow, zigger-zigger,
as happiness clicks upwards like a score.

I run down the abstract alleyways
past the white bips of power, the gun-metal
balconies where you can have combats
if that's what you're into. I continue
through explosions, through 'you're dead, buster',
for surely I'm dying already, straight through
each phantasm of power: Germany
can't challenge me, Japan, the US,
these obvious villains with
bulging thighs and unbelievable sneers.

Before GAME OVER in this figured world,
I look for the real world's beauty,
waiting by a wicker gate, as in older stories.
Were I a flesh woman she'd be a man,
for she's ordinary, not particular to me,
and wears different gowns in various seasons
of this tryst. I am heart-worn to see her
face that looks pained, starved, flinching
at bombs, or cackling with laughter,
someone the game can't idealise.

I love her so truly she multiplies
into millions, warm, crowding, hungry
in their nations, as if her image were
jiggered by time-lapses into histories.

94

She waits for any sincere person
to penetrate this strangeness we've created
and to become flesh with her flesh.
She points her hand to me and on to her finger
I slip the black diamond, Africa,
which I found in a tiny country, Botswana.

Congo/Zaire: Rich, Became Poor

Patrice Lumumba, the captivating orator who had become first premier of the newly-independent Congo, had been in office only 19 days when, on July 19, 1960, the U.S. Ambassador in Brussels, William Burden, cabled the US government in reply to a query. Lumumba was trying to hold a federal government together against separatist movements in Katanga, the rich mineral mining district. Burden gave this dangerous leftist absolutely no chance, but immediately called for US measures to restore stability out of anarchy and to salvage a Western entrée into the Congo. His cable said Lumumba had:

> MANEUVERED HIMSELF INTO POSITION OF OPPOSITION TO WEST, RESISTANCE TO UNITED NATIONS AND INCREASING DEPENDENCE ON SOVIET UNION AND ON CONGOLESE SUPPORTERS (KASHAMURA, GIZENGA) WHO ARE PURSUING SOVIET ENDS.

Burden went on to recommend:

> ONLY PRUDENT, THEREFORE, TO PLAN ON BASIS THAT LUMUMBA GOVERNMENT THREATENS OUR VITAL INTERESTS IN CONGO AND AFRICA GENERALLY. A PRINCIPAL OBJECTIVE OF OUR POLITICAL AND DIPLOMATIC ACTION MUST THEREFORE BE TO DESTROY LUMUMBA GOVERNMENT AS NOW CONSTITUTED, BUT AT THE SAME TIME WE MUST FIND OR DEVELOP ANOTHER HORSE TO BACK WHICH WOULD BE ACCEPTABLE IN REST OF AFRICA AND DEFENSIBLE AGAINST SOVIET POLITICAL ATTACK.
>
> [See: MADELEINE G. KALB, *The Congo Cables: The Cold War in Africa – from Eisenhower to Kennedy* (NY: Macmillan, 1982).

That "other horse" turned out to be Marshal Mobutu Sese Seko, the fearsome and long-lasting dictator who emerged out of the wreck of Congolese politics in the 1960s. He renamed the country, Zaire.

For the next three decades Zaire's wealth was bled out by bribery, corruption, and terror tactics, amounting to a system of mutual dependence beginning at the highest levels of government and reaching down to the most lowly official or soldier. Exactly because so many were involved, this network held the starved-out nation precariously together. Mobutu became increasingly isolated internationally and tried to rehabilitate himself by accepting Hutu refugees from Rwanda, who crowded into camps on Zaire's border hills, adding to the country's burdens.

In a final twist of fate, an ailing Mobutu was ousted by a former Lumumba supporter, Laurent Kabila, and the nation's name reverted to the Democratic Republic of Congo. The CIA reportedly backed Kabila against Mobutu but didn't know what do when Kabila's forces got to Kinshasa. For Kabila had looked the other way when his troops, heavily boosted by soldiers from Tutsi-run Rwanda, massacred Hutu refugees in the Congo's jungles – a Tutsi revenge for the Hutu-led genocide in their own country.

The Kabila regime immediately had to confront rebels in the east with help from Hutu militias and local Congolese, especially the Mayi-Mayi. Angola, Chad, Namibia and Zimbabwe backed him. Uganda and Rwanda (with Angola wavering) now provide troops for the rebel Congolese Rally for Democracy because Kabila cannot cut Congo supply routes for their own enemies: Uganda's rebel Lord's Resistance Army, the Rwandan Hutus, and Unita in Angola. In an enormously complex political breakdown, other countries which, for a variety of motives, have taken military action include Burundi and, reportedly, Sudan.

In all this the Congo's mineral wealth is the magnet. What could be a great central African nation offers sharp business opportunities for neighbours who manage to place themselves favourably. As peace talks stumble, this vital central tract of Africa could yet blunder further into a multi-national war. The UN is planning to send a miniscule peacekeeping force.

From a Dark Hill in Paris

I sit on the dark hill where I often sit
to reflect on these nations, but not grandiosely;
I'm just a pale figure leaning
his head against a bare branch caught
by a gleam from the ludicrous half moon
vibrant above evergreen forests below me, say
the great river basin of the Zaire, and I haven't got
political, only private thoughts of the well-wisher.
I cast an old glove down into the Congo; it freefalls
   je
ga
in negative down the precipice, not a challenge,
not a gage but an empty handshake, oh-oh.

It falls into marshes with rushes bent bodily
by strong currents rippling through, islets
of ant-hills covered with dura, antelopes
plunging into elephant footprints, emerging
streaming with water under pelting rain.
Puffs of papyrus, arums, fish with jaw hooks
to grapple plants while they feed, the rivers
spreading out into broad friths and sponges.
This is unnatural, for my hill is Montmartre,
yet rushes are strawed with oil-yellow light
   je
ga
not entirely mentally healthy, more a foreboding,
in a mental vignette, like Millet cornfields, oh-oh.

There'd been one moment sprinkled by butterflies,
a June Day in Léopoldville, when a Belgian king
handed over the nation, yet tactlessly
praised Léopold, king of atrocity, whose mansions
were paid for by a currency of severed hands;
and Lumumba at the rostrum of Congolese unity
turned on King Baudouin: 'The Congo's
wounds are too fresh to forget': a true word.
And this was Day One. Lumumba
turned from the rostrum to a nation already divided,

Day 5, an army in mutiny because Belgium
broke promises, then instantly plotted with Tshombe,
who, Day 11, pulled Katanga out of the Union,
    je
ga
Katanga rich in cobalt, fee'd to Belgium and Britain,
uranium source for Hiroshima, source for Tshombe, oh-oh.

Night huffs its shadows, mane-shaped bushes
occlude the river-basin from me while I listen
to the babble of Sacré-Cœur tourists behind me.
Khrushchev wooed the Congolese premier; Tshombe
wooed the Belgians; by Day 49
the US were planning to kill Lumumba.
Below under Paris moonshine a ferris wheel
comes suddenly alight by the river and starts turning,
and dot men in suits are running for their lives
in 1961 while men in battledress
slowly take those lives. I'm not seeing this;
it's seeing me though the soldiers don't look at my hill.
There flashes into mind the bloody pout of a beaten man
    je
ga
manhandled by Tshombe's soldiers;
it's Lumumba; he's passed out of history, oh-oh.

On a hot night in August, a trash-can on Montmartre
exudes the urinous smell of human decay:
below in the forests, the brown river flows onwards
hidden by trees taller than buildings, a Zaire
never to know peace after that, for they'd torn
the Congo body apart; the UN in its hauteur,
Khrushchev and Kennedy playing with the world.
The ferris wheel stops, dulls in grey daylight,
a remote window in darkness beyond evergreen trees;
it's a minehead pulley in Katanga, depressing rain
mists the elected premier of new independence,
dying like that, speeches glistening on his voluble tongue.
    je
ga
Lumumba delivered to his enemies
down in Katanga, as the US knew well, oh-oh.

A word, *kwashiorkor*, comes to me like a rumour.
I turn down my lookout hill and thread through
tourists, towards my road home, rue Lepic.
It's as if I'd heard traffic murmuring the word
in the Seine's river darkness, in the hubbub
from refugee multitudes on Kivu's hills where
denuded Rwandans huddle under their blue
UN tents; so my walking can't be free, can't be
spendthrift. The wealthy of Europe pass by me.
I know the starved body feeds off its muscles,
and I brood on the Congo: kwashiorkor amid riches,
    je
ga
Cholera waves its skeleton wand by Kivu Lake, island tops
are starred with palms, things are drifting apart, oh-oh.

South Africa

A Kenyan author, Ali A. Mazrui, put forward some time ago a bizarre proposal for healing Africa's wounds. Recolonisation – but with a difference.

To heal countries like Liberia or Somalia, where order has disintegrated, he suggests a system of trusteeships somewhat like the controversial UN mandate over the Congo in 1960 but this time more genuinely international and less Western. Administering powers for the trusteeship territories might come from Africa or the UN. For example the Organisation of African Unity might have to intervene under this Pax Africana in countries that are out of control.

One of his ideas is to have five regional states selected to oversee the continent and to act as future anchors of stability – he is thinking of the future and deliberately ignores their present problems which I have noted in parentheses:

> North region, Egypt, Algeria (rent by Islamic faction);
> West, Nigeria (oil-rich but politically still reconstructing; see below for
>   Nigeria participation in ECOMOG forces in Sierra Leone);
> East, either Ethiopia (now at war again) or Kenya (fairly stable,
>   but authoritarian);
> Centre, Congo/Zaire (see previous section);
> South, South Africa (whose future is so chancy but which has been
>   playing somewhat of the role Mazrui suggests).

They would form an African Security Council, with a Pan-African army at its disposal for emergency peacekeeping. There would also be an African High Commissioner for Refugees linked to the UN refugee agency. Half of the world's refugees are in Africa, he points out. Thus in the 21st century Ethiopia, assuming a return to peace there, might become a benign, controlling trustee on the UN's behalf for Somalia (at present virtually ungovernable), or Egypt for Sudan (undergoing civil war), or South Africa for Angola (the civil war has renewed).

Whether warring nations would submit to trusteeship is beyond me. UN trusteeship of the Congo/Zaire is a particularly unhappy example as Professor Mazrui, a distinguished historian, would know. In practice, African peacekeeping may either be beneficent (examples are hard to find) or, as in the present Congo where there are potential business advantages for "friendly" nations, may carry risk of new wars.

The only truly African peacekeeping force was the 15,000 ECOMOG force aiding the legitimate Sierra Leone government against rebels. France, Britain, the US, and Denmark nowadays stress that African peacekeeping should be strengthened but the UN plans to reduce its presence on the continent, making the indigenous task more difficult.

Yet Africa is potentially rich: it has the world's largest reserve of arable land, and its raw material riches extend from the oil fields of the Nigeria, to the copper veins that run through Zambia, to the minerals in Congo/Zaire, to the diamonds in South Africa, Botswana, or Angola.

Development philosophy has been changing fast. The World Bank is less keen on 'big aid' to the Third World. The Bank's latest president, James D. Wolfensohn, has talked of reducing the Bank's role as a funder of major development projects, which critics have charged help neither the environment nor the poor. Instead he would have it functioning more as a consultant for private capital to flow into developing countries.

Ideally, aid should help nomads to remain nomads, pygmies to remain pygmies, ancient river management to become more efficient rather than be drowned out by dams, and existing cropping or animal husbandry to become more efficient. Untrammelled global trading, transnational activity, and genetic engineering of new species may make such hopes seem romantic.

But on a small scale, very positive results have been reported for village loan schemes, or 'micro-aid'. In a Gambian case, loan sums as low as $30 have been enough for about 60 village women to set up their own businesses and revive a whole village. The loans and interest income can then be recycled within the village like a rotating credit system. In Mali, a scheme among the Dogon has surpassed organisers' expectations, unlocking undreamt of savings and repayment capacity in a disadvantaged region. Microcredit proponents have ambitiously set targets to reach 100 million of the world's 1.6 billion poorest families by the year 2005, and Africa, where so far only about 1.2 million are enrolled, seems the most fertile field of all.

By keying in with local economies, Micro-credit might prove a socially-sensitive seeding for larger-scale growth, especially if carried out with UN participation.

In another proposal, the former South African President F.W. de Klerk suggests that the international community should allow African exports to enter international markets on favourable terms, and that primary exports should have value added to them before they leave Africa. That same community should attend to key countries in each of the main regions as development partners (here, his plan has affinity with Mazrui's).

We are not to dream of magic solutions. For good or ill, African countries will undergo 'evolution, not revolution', as conservatives love to say. But the international consequences of leaving a whole continent largely deprived are frightening to contemplate.

One large-scale example of where free-market philosophy could save a country would surely be the new South Africa. The ANC has come to power aware that a cash-starved socialist regime cannot succeed against international capitalism – a hard-won wisdom.

What are we to make of these remarks by Meg Voorhes of the Investor Responsibility Research Center, a US group monitoring trade with South Africa? She was saying transnationals can serve the South Africa market 'with goods produced elsewhere' and added: 'South Africa is not seen as a major sourcing point for exporting globally.'

That would mean penetration of the South African economy from outside without genuine stimulation of domestic production. It is the voice of deregulation speaking. This, at a time when Black South Africans are trying to move more firmly into business.

Anglo American Corp., a huge mining conglomerate, is moving its headquarters to London in a merger move because it needs more access to capital than is available in South Africa's market. Once again, global trading drives this move. The conglomerate claims that it will feed employment and investment back to South Africa: the South African government agrees, while the Congress of South African Trade Unions has called it a vote of no confidence in the home country.

Foreign investment in South Africa blows hot and cold. A single negative article in *The Wall Street Journal* is enough to dip its markets, as investors worldwide hurry to safer havens. The unions could wreck these balances if they are too irresponsible at such a delicate time. Complaints from external investors include that South Africa's unionised workers are too "uppity" and strike-prone. In Southeast Asia labour costs are cheaper, skills are higher, and there's more company loyalty, said a Japanese economics attaché. Apparently, the transnationals don't like wages of $5 an hour, a pittance for Westerners.

I don't presume to say what workers should get. But a strong South Africa is essential to the health of Africa long-term. What then, if its economy continues to look a dubious investment to Western financiers and transnationals? Where is the long-term financial support for genuinely beneficial South African policies going to come from?

In practice, transnational executives can look no longer-term than the reasonable return on an investment to satisfy shareholders. If, as is quite likely, international firms look elsewhere than to South Africa – to Asian labour at near-slave wages, say – then the spirit of colonialism that we thought we had laid to rest will live on in the necessities of the financial balance sheet.

The Toe of a Continent

The toe of a continent has been dipped into hope
while the body is covered with slashes and bruises,
the little countries gaping with wounds:
Liberia savage in wars where once was freedom;
Freetown ideals spent out in Sierra Leone;
Rwanda entering history as a monument
to genocide, to French interference
and inter-tribal blindness. The centre
of Africa ravaged. After the murderous
dictators, the torture cells, the hard-hearted
arrogant coups, the lie of the single party,
its necessity never proved;
and after the brilliant leftists, proud
to invent solutions, shunting their people
into co-operative villages and into worse poverty;
after euphoria of independence
used to create power for bloody-handed soldiers;
after the panicky flight of white money,
the desperate loans welcomed at first
at over-high interests, never a gift,
but the banks piling debts on drowning nations;
then after the closing of banking privileges,
after it all – the cadences of Auden –
after slaughter of families –
we can never imagine the scale of it –
desperately we imagine a river of hope still runs,
and the Northern banks will respond.

At the foot of this poem lies South Africa,
dipped into hope, where traitorous whites
have already started shifting out money,
and global investors withhold their starter funds,
but where Mandela, untrembling,
his toe in the black river, waded deeper
into hope for this whole continent,
like someone finally baptised into a faith
more equal, more ancient than Christianity.

Who will provide such a priceless balm?
What industrial nation, able to pay
a part of the sum, will end our betrayal?
How slowly evil plots in darkness
away from such rivers. How quickly
South Africa changed when it changed.
How little the poem can know.

Aid: Payback Time

By this year 2000, four-fifths of the world population are said to be living in developing countries.

As I bring this book to an end, I have been expressing delight that the world's rich countries are waking up (somewhat) to the need for more help. Debt forgiveness is one of the hottest international topics; World Bank lending is to be topped up by $11 billion over the next three years; and the OECD is developing a 20-year plan to help developing nations. We have seen how Britain, Europe, and the US have vowed to give the continent special attention.

This belated recognition justifies an unusual poetry book attempted in the face of a post-Larkin, British poetic culture which sniffs at too much literary ambition. I have risked overreaching because poets should not fear trying to respond to the complexity of their real lives.

As I have been implying all along, part of that complexity is that I am in debt to Africa – so are my fellow citizens in the three countries I have worked in, Britain, France, and the US. Modestly as we may try to live, we have all got richer off the back of world poverty and are still doing so. It's not just a question of compassion; we have been breaking the tacit contract the rich always owe to the poor. The debt mounts daily.

The Cold Hotel

On the ticket to fantasy lands
we find the cold hotel whose door
is opened by the key of Europe.
If we could only find that key
(and the management is searching)
we'd enter a comfy bedroom with
a Euromoney terminal,
rented armchairs, wide mattress;
and when we ordered
tea or coffee from room service,
it'd come up with plenty of sugars,
the way it did when our incomes
were acquired from slavery's aftermath
across Africa, India, the Caribbean,
in all the unsavoury histories of
our island pride.

Nothing has been fantasy
in African lands for writers jailed and exiled
under regimes we helped to spawn.
The great ambassadors:
Kofi Awoonor, Ezekiel Mphahlele,
Frank Chipasula, Dennis Brutus,
Arthur Nortje, Ngugi wa Thiong'o.

I go beyond my rights to name such names,
myself a travelling poet-representative
for a people that won't take a dip
in their incomes, no not for any
possible good imaginable,
not for any benefit of the future's poor,
not even for their own grandchildren.

Can this really be our room key?
It just fits our suitcase locks.
Inside the case are Stephen King's Gothic
novels from many airports, little thrillers,
and another country's currency bills
financing the circle that maintains us,

a geometry mystical as the Catholic God,
comfortably horrific
whose island centre is nowhere
but whose deregulated circumference
passes clearly through that hotel room in
Brussels, Stuttgart, Bonn.

We live in
an illusion that we'd face horror
well if it ever came to us.

Paris: the Kora

Just as my project was beginning, here in Paris, I took the Métro from my old Montmartre flat through the 19th arrondissement to the mildly dangerous station of Stalingrad, whose warren of tunnels is often unpoliced late on Sunday.

An Arabian North African picked my pocket. He stood suspiciously near Alice on a long escalator, looked vaguely villainous, and moved two steps upwards when I stared him out; so I clamped my hand on my wallet which I had unwisely put in my trouser pocket. At the top he dropped his cigarette packet and, to keep still, marked time furiously on the metal stairs as if trying to retrieve it. Though I could see the trick of it, the escalator instantly barged me against his sturdy buttocks and my hands went wide to regain my balance. Bent over like that in his odd dance he robbed me intimately from in front, reaching back and into my trouser pocket. Without time to pass the wallet to a waiting accomplice, he took off fast as I puffed after him down the gleaming warren shouting, *'Voleur!'*

A tiny criminal sub-culture has centred itself on Stalingrad Métro and its escalator. In one year, I saw six attempts at pick-pocketing there. This thief must have snorted to find my wallet empty of all but credit cards, and hurled the contents away in disgust. The following day, a Martiniquais computer engineer brought my driving licence to my door and four days later one of my ID documents was mailed to me by an African nun.

The inner Eastern ring of Paris from Belleville through Stalingrad to Barbès forms a hinterland of Arabia- and Africa-in-exile within the heart of Paris. The handful of pickpockets contributes to the Parisians' perception of this inner area as prone to crime and drugs, and a vicious back-street trade in crack doesn't help. Murderous tension in Algeria between Islamic fundamentalists and the French-backed regime have sometimes added to the bias against North Africans back in Paris. Worse, one year Islamic terrorists riposted with bombs on the Métro and in French streets.

Paris itself divides the races, intensifies prejudice, and banishes immigrants to the ghettos or poorer suburbs. Yet most inner city households depend upon North Africans to staff corner stores that stay open long after French-run supermarkets. Parisians forget the liveliness of their city's Arabian or African streets compared with the leaden dullness of rich, white Neuilly barricaded behind security devices. Small ethnic groups from countries north and south of the Sahara crowd into these eastern streets and into the outer suburbs, clinging on to something of their old cultures. If Chinese diaspora capital has now invaded the Belleville district, it was long the Maghrebian couscous capital and the jewel shops there still hang with as many gold ornaments as an African-American shop in Brooklyn. There is a busy life of Muslim prayer rooms.

From high up in apartment blocks, African marabout magicians send their friends out to distribute fliers in the Métro promising love, wealth and happiness. These are not usually the grand marabouts of Islam, the religious leaders who sometimes come across from their own countries to make celebrity visits to Parisian mosques; these are only linkmen with the spiritual life of the homeland, some of them inauthentic and living on their wits in the foreign city.

African holy-roller Christians have a chapel off Pigalle just down from where I used to live. You can go to the Paris-Dakar café in the 10th arrondissement or to the Tontine d'Or in the 11th and listen to the *griot* poet-musicians of Senegal and Gambia twanging their koras while they chant the Islamic praise songs of their native lands, adaptable for praising tourists too. In Paris, often, you are led to think about Africa.

The Herb

Primavera curtains hide the false Professor
in his Parisian apartment. His aides
hand out ads at the Metro, promising
detailed success in love and life.

Upstairs, I'm told, behind Barbès or Place Clichy,
there's some tiny room where heavies
stare at you while advice is murmured
through the thin cotton hangings.

Fictive happiness often hides inside shells
like a dawn cockerel hiding in a grotto,
or finger ends of chamois leather gloves
inside mussels clinging to the groin of magical practice.

An under-life of sorcery among crowds
round iridescent fabric shops
fronting poorer streets, an islanded culture
in darkened marshes of Parisian autochthones.

You will pay for his journey to somewhere in Africa;
he has to get a herb that guarantees your marriage
will take place as a silken lie, your partner's tongue
turned in the mouth to yellow cloth.

Grown newly nasty, the French police
are chasing down the magician's life with demands
for IDs made greasy in garages of failed employment
shit-scared illegal taps scam.

The *terre d'asile* is crossed by beak-winged birds,
fetish shadows that pass through the worst dreams
as a false-winged word may cast shadow on a marriage
or magic become fugitive in a culture

transposed onto foreign soil, magic as a calling card
placed in your mailbox, a means of survival,
half in French, half in Arabic.
And none of us did this, none of us allowed this to happen.

NOTES

I haven't wanted to burden poems with a lengthy bibliography. I gratefully acknowledge the help of all the many authorities and journalists whose work I have consulted but not cited. Sources in my original manuscript most directly referred to are as follows.

Shyam Bhatia: 'L'esclavage ressuscité', translation of an article originally in *The Observer*, in *Courrier International*, 27 April to 3 May 1995.

Renée Chao-Béroff: 'Developing Financial Services in Poor Regions: Self-Managed Village Savings and Loan Associations in the Dogon Region of Mali', in Hartmut Schneider (ed.), *MicroFinance for the Poor?* (Paris: Development Centre of the OECD, 1997).

Philip D. Curtin (ed.) et al: *Africa Remembered: Narratives by West Africans from the Era of the Slave Trade* (Madison: University of Wisconsin Press, 1968).

E.E. Evans-Pritchard: *Witchcraft, Oracles and Magic among the Azande*, (Oxford: Oxford University Press, 1937).

Richard Hakluyt: *Voyages* (London: Dent, Everyman, 1962 reprint of 1907 edition).

Jeremy Harding: 'The Partisan', review of Basil Davidson, *The Search for Africa: A History in the Making* in *London Review of Books*, 23 June 1994, pp.15-19.

Stimela Jason Jingoes: *A Chief Is a Chief by the People*, recorded and compiled by John and Cassandra Perry (London: Oxford University Press, 1975).

Madeleine G. Kalb: *The Congo Cables: The Cold War in Africa – from Eisenhower to Kennedy* (NY: Macmillan Publishing, 1982).

Anthony Lewis: 'A Gloomy Vision of Anarchy Sweeping the World', *International Herald Tribune*, 7 March 1994.

David Livingstone: *The Last Journals of David Livingstone, in Central Africa, from 1865 to His Death*, ed. Horace Waller, 2 vols (London: John Murray, 1880).

Jerry Mander & Edward Goldsmith: *The Case Against the Global Economy and For a Turn Toward the Local* (San Francisco: Sierra Club Books, 1996).

Jack Mapanje: 'Bitter-sweet Tears: Letter from Malawi', *Index on Censorship*, 2 (1995).

Rob Nixon: 'Pipe-Dreams', review of Ken Saro-Wiwa, *A Month and a Day: A Detention Diary* in *London Review of Books*, 4 April 1996.

Marguerite Roby: *My Adventures in the Congo* (London: Edward Arnold, 1911).

Robert I. Rotberg: *The Rise of Nationalism in Central Africa: The Making of Malawi and Zambia, 1873-1964* (Cambridge, Mass: Harvard University Press, 1965).

Stanlake Samkange: *Origins of Rhodesia* (London: Heinemann Educational Books, 1968). Moffat quotations taken by Samkange from *Matebele Journal of Robert Moffat*, ed. J.R.P. Wallis (Chatto and Windus 1945).

George Shepperson & Thomas Price: *Independent African: John Chilembwe and the Origins, Setting and Significance of the Nyasaland Native Rising of 1915* (Edinburgh: Edinburgh University Press, 1958).

Wole Soyinka: 'A Brutal Feudal Minority May Be Destroying Nigeria', *International Herald Tribune*, 23 August 1994.

Wole Soyinka: 'The General's Nightmare,' *Newsweek*, 26 June 1995.

Robert Farris Thompson: *Flash of the Spirit: African & Afro-American Art & Philosophy* (NY: Vintage, 1984).

Alice Walker & Pratibha Parmar: *Warrior Marks: Female Genital Mutilation and the Sexual Blinding of Women* (NY: Harcourt Brace & Co., 1993).

Sir Alan Walters, '2000: Britain Can Go from Strength to Strength', *Daily Mail*, 17 December 1993.

William Shawcross: *Murdoch* (London: Chatto & Windus, 1992).

Harold Wilson: *The Labour Government, 1964-1970* (London: Weidenfeld, 1971).